THE ULTIMATE INTERIORS BOOK

WOOD

Jane Struthers

EP

EBURY PRESS
LONDON

For Bill

First published 1991 by Ebury Press
an imprint of the Random Century Group
Random Century House
20 Vauxhall Bridge Road
London SW1V 2SA

Design: The Image
Picture research: Gabrielle Allen

Front jacket photograph by Chris Mead
Back jacket photograph by Debbie Patterson

British Library Cataloguing in Publication Data
Struthers, Jane
Wood: The ultimate interiors book –
from Colonial to Shaker, a sourcebook
of decorative ideas.
I. Title
749.2

ISBN 0-7126-4893-3

Typeset in Bembo by Tek Art Ltd,
Addiscombe, Croydon, Surrey
Printed and bound in Italy by
New Interlitho S.p.a., Milan

Contents

Introduction

The thread running through the whole history of furniture and most architecture, whether one talks about the Ancient Egyptians, French Baroque, American Shaker or English Jacobean, is wood. It has always been the preferred material for building, especially in the past when there were so many more forests, and craftsmen had ready supplies of cheap timber to hand. They could whittle small logs or branches into tiny boxes, kitchen equipment, gifts for their loved ones or toys for their children; huge pieces of oak were used to make the timber frames of houses; piles of elm were buried in rivers to make solid bridges; and planks of oak, elm or whatever hardwood was to hand could be sawn up to make furniture. As world travel increased new woods were discovered and imported, or saplings were brought home to see if they would grow in a new environment.

The history of a country's furniture is inseparable from its social history: the times when the furniture becomes heavily decorated and highly ornate signify eras of prosperity, while the years when the style of furniture becomes simpler and less showy indicate times of comparative hardship, or even war. Furniture also signifies the prevailing mood of the time: until the seventeenth century, when French furniture moved into the ascendant, the effects of the Italian Renaissance had been felt throughout every country in Europe, and furniture was deemed to be an indication of its owner's learning and appreciation of art. The Puritans, on the other hand, also had an impact on styles of furniture, which became plainer, sturdier and much more sober. The Shakers continued this style in America, producing furniture that reflected their way of life and their codes of conduct.

There has always been a difference between country furniture (which, until its current vogue was only bought by the people for whom it was intended) and the showier, so-called important pieces bought by the wealthier classes. Indeed, until the sixteenth century such items as chairs were real indicators of class and birth, and anyone who wasn't a member of the nobility or aristocracy had to make do instead with a simple stool or bench.

A brief history of furniture

It is fascinating to study the history of furniture, and there are many interesting books devoted to the subject. What follows here is a selective history, concentrating on the major movements and influences in France, Britain and America from 1600 to the beginning of the twentieth century. The illustrations in the rest of this book also cover this period.

It is only during the past four hundred years that furniture has changed considerably. Before then, early medieval furniture was made mostly for practical purposes – it was completely functional and had little decoration. Life for many people was very unsettled, so furniture had to be simple and easily moved from one place to another. Tables were of the trestle variety and could be swiftly dismantled. Chairs were a rarity – most people made do with uncomfortable stools or benches that could be pushed against the wall whenever a back rest was needed.

This magnificent French commode has drawers inlaid with marquetry and a marble top. Ornate gilt handles create a sense of flamboyance, which is further enhanced by the pair of blackamoors standing guard on either side. Pieces of furniture like this show the rich legacy left by French furniture through the centuries.

It was the Renaissance that started the fashion for different styles of furniture. Its aim was to return to classical styles and ideals, and its influence swiftly spread from its birthplace in Italy across Europe. The decorative arts flowered as never before; painters discovered how to capture perspective on canvas (which cabinet-makers then transferred to furniture with the use of inlays and marquetry); and beauty was a byword. Furniture in Italy, Spain, Portugal, France, the Low Countries, Germany, Austria and Scandinavia grew considerably in sophistication. However, it must be said that English designers were not quite such wholehearted converts, but they were in the grip of the Reformation and the continuing quarrel with the Catholic Church that had been started by Henry VIII.

The influence of France

Until the middle of the seventeenth century the Italian Baroque style had been the predominating European influence, but then the first signs of change appeared. The Gobelin family's tapestry workshops were bought by Colbert, Louis XIV's prime minister in 1662, and were converted five years later into the *Manufacture royale des meubles de la Couronne*. It was committed to glorifying the reign of the Sun King and one result was the Louis XIV style of furniture, heavily influenced by the ornate Baroque style but with fewer curves, more straight lines and a great deal of bold carving. Among the new pieces of furniture that evolved during this time were the commode or chest of drawers, and the console table. Veneering and marquetry (inlay work) were increasingly popular.

After Louis XIV died the pomp and splendour of his Versailles court gradually diminished until it became the elegant Rococo style of Louis XV. This was heavily influenced by oriental art, which was being discovered following the opening up of the trade routes to the East. Curves were back in fashion and the flower was the favourite motif, carved on the legs of chairs and appearing in marquetry. Console tables, beds, desks and chairs are among the important pieces of the time.

By the time Louis XVI came to the throne in 1774 there was a general feeling against the Baroque and Rococo styles and a move towards simpler, classic lines which became the Neoclassic style. Curves vanished and were replaced with straight lines, and decorations used geometric marquetry or white and gold paint. Even so, the furniture itself was sumptuous and was made by highly skilled craftsmen. This era has been called the golden age of cabinet-making, and Louis XVI furniture was sold to foreign royalty and aristocracy. It was even popular in Britain, where the Adam style predominated.

Something else that was predominating in France was social unrest, which culminated in the French Revolution of 1789 and the short-lived republican government known as the Directoire. The vogue for the classical style continued, but furniture was also modelled on English designs of the period. Strict, military styles took over from 1800, when Napoleon Bonaparte took control of the Directoire government and of France. During this Empire period designs became much more sober; for example, upholstered chairs with rectangular backs replaced those with scroll backs.

Between 1814 and 1870 (the Restoration and the Second Empire), French furniture style was unremarkable, save for the mechanized production techniques that were emerging in the furniture industry. The next major furniture style arrived with the Art Nouveau period, which proliferated across Europe and lasted from about 1885 to 1910, and which was a reaction against the burgeoning industrialization and the paucity of good design. Sweeping curves and decorative motifs borrowed from nature, such as birds, flowers and fish, abounded.

The famous Paris exhibition of 1925 for *les Arts Décoratifs* spawned Art Deco, which bore a superficial resemblance to Cubism with its squares, triangles and circles. Many of the furniture styles of the time are still acting as inspiration for designers today.

English furniture

Furniture styles varied little from Elizabethan designs during the reigns of the early Stuart kings, James I and Charles I. Items were mostly made of oak in a rectangular design, but had less decoration than before. Chests developed into early chests of drawers; stools were given backs, and known as backstools.

Furniture design was suitably sombre during the period of the Cromwells, from 1649–60, but once Charles II came to the throne it enjoyed the same blossoming as was taking place in the court of Louis XIV in France. The Baroque style flourished, walnut was commonly used and carving proliferated, with decorated chair backs and legs. Chairs became more comfortable.

During the reign of William and Mary, after 1685, when the Protestant religion was forbidden in France, the arrival in Britain of huge numbers of Huguenot craftsmen had a marvellous effect on furniture styles. Distilled versions of Baroque furniture were produced

and oriental lacquered furniture became immensely popular, due to the increasing trade with the East. Japanning (a technique using black varnish) was introduced to cope with the demand, and chests and cabinets were frequently made in this way.

The Queen Anne period (1702–14) was one of the most graceful in English furniture. English design had been dominated for some time by continental ideas, designs and craftsmen, so a complete assimilation of these influences, plus a revival of the long-standing dislike of anything French, spawned the Queen Anne style. Pieces were small and elegant, often finished with figured walnut veneering and given decorative feet. The furniture reflected Britain's growing prosperity and the increasing leisure enjoyed by the ever-expanding middle class. Chairs continued to develop – the spoon-back chair was a product of this period – with the accent on further comfort, and card tables were produced as a mania for gambling swept the country. Small tea tables and stands also appeared, because food, drink and entertaining were attracting great attention.

The Palladian movement under George I and George II (1714–60) marked a return to classical values and ideals, and acted as a forerunner to the Neoclassical movement in France. Mahogany replaced walnut as the favoured wood and the Queen Anne style was modified considerably. The furniture was Baroque to a marked degree, with large-scale sculptural ornamentation and astonishingly florid gilded pieces. This was mostly due to William Kent, who was the first British architect to design furniture specifically for his buildings. He was strongly influenced by Inigo Jones, and his furniture (which was immensely heavy) had an architectural quality. It was also arranged in symmetrical patterns in a room.

Rococo style swiftly took over and dominated British furniture by the 1750s, but it was less elaborate and extravagant than its French counterpart. Pattern books ensured the Rococo style spread up and down the country. Thomas Chippendale published one of the most influential pattern books, with the result that the Rococo style flourished in Britain and America. Chippendale's furniture was made of mahogany and some styles are still named for him today, such as Chinese Chippendale which was influenced by oriental designs, and Chippendale Gothic, which heralded the Neo-Gothic style that was yet to come.

The Neoclassical revival spread to Britain from France during the 1760s and received considerable encouragement from the Scots architect Robert Adam, who always dictated the style of the interiors of his buildings. He worked primarily with satinwood and fruitwoods, decorating his pieces with inlay and marquetry (see pages 30–31). The work of George Hepplewhite is also linked with Neoclassicism of 1780–90. Only his pattern books survive, but they show how he softened the Adam look with gentle curves, particularly with bow and serpentine fronts. He enjoyed using japanning and marquetry, and his favourite wood was satinwood. Hepplewhite's style was very well known in America, where his pattern books had a great influence on Federal furniture.

Thomas Sheraton was another cabinet-maker whose pattern books ensured his everlasting fame. He liked flat inlaid or painted decoration, especially banding and parquetry, and his square-back chairs serve as hallmarks of his work. He was also very influential in America and made his mark on Federal furniture.

Regency style followed, and used forms and decoration borrowed from ancient Egyptian, Greek and Roman furniture, as well as elements of contemporary French and Chinese furniture. It was a very restrained look, and the most prominent exponent was Thomas Hope, whose pattern books included pieces inspired by the French Empire and Directoire styles.

A strong sense of tradition marked the Victorian period, which was characterized by rather heavy, solid furniture. The Regency style was still prominent early in Victoria's reign, but various revivals soon developed and, with their strong decorations and eclectic features, soon characterized this period. The growth of the Industrial Revolution meant that furniture could now be mass-produced for the increasing numbers of people who wanted to buy it. The immensely influential Arts and Crafts Movement developed as a reaction to this, based on the ideas of John Ruskin and William Morris, who called for a return to the pre-industrial methods of production. Furniture design returned to simpler styles, with a reduction in excessive decoration and use of simple, traditional materials. A taste for the medieval spawned the Neo-Gothic Movement, started by AWN Pugin, but this was directed towards industrial design rather than a return to the hand-craft methods of the past.

The Arts and Crafts Movement had a strong impact on the Art Nouveau style, which followed. In Britain, the Scots architect Charles Rennie Mackintosh and his circle, known as the Glasgow School, were inspired by ancient Celtic calligraphy to produce furniture that is still influential today. Many of the designs were

produced by Ambrose Heal for sale in his shop, Heals.

The influence of America

Early settlers in America took their own furniture with them, imported from their native countries, but this soon had to be abandoned because the new climate made the pieces shrink and crack. Transporting furniture across the country was impractical, so both craftsmen and unskilled men made their own furniture from local materials – often oak and maple – using the pattern books they had taken with them. They were of necessity less elaborate than the originals and were quite bulky. Named after two of the Pilgrim Fathers, Brewster and Carver chairs were both very popular,

The sitting room at Charleston Farmhouse, near Lewes in Sussex, is a veritable portfolio of the work of painters Vanessa Bell and Duncan Grant, who lived here. Virtually every surface has been painted, with the happy exception of the walnut glass-fronted cabinet in the corner.

made from turned ash, maple, hickory or elm, with rush seats. The Carver chair was a model for many seventeenth-century Colonial designers.

The popularity of walnut throughout Europe spread to America at the beginning of the eighteenth century, where it was used to create furniture that was less bulky and more ornamental. The cabriole leg was introduced and marquetry and painting were both used to decorate furniture. The tallboy, a tall chest with five or six tiers of drawers, was introduced at this time.

The American Queen Anne period lasted from 1714–60. Mahogany was now being used in addition to walnut, maple and pine, and the formal styles of William and Mary gave way to the curved elegance of the Queen Anne style.

A variety of imported styles, such as early Georgian, Gothic and the Chinese and Rococo styles of mid-eighteenth-century Britain, characterized the American Chippendale period (1755–85). Cabinet-makers in Philadelphia developed a restrained distillation of Chippendale's designs from his pattern books. Mahogany was still in the ascendant.

The American War of Independence inevitably gave rise to antipathy for Britain. When communications were re-established in 1775 the Sheraton and Hepplewhite styles were at the forefront of British furniture design. Scots-born cabinet-maker Duncan Phyfe specialized in Sheraton furniture in New York City and was the principal creator of American Empire style, which was based on elements borrowed from the French Empire style and the British Regency style. Large, bold pieces of furniture were given curves and rounded corners, and decorated with figured veneering.

During the Federal period, which lasted from the 1790s to the 1830s, the prevailing influences on American design gradually shifted from such late Adam exponents as Sheraton and Hepplewhite to the Directoire and Empire styles of France. Increasing amounts of French furniture were being imported into America, and many French craftsmen had emigrated there. Federal furniture was less ornate than its continental counterparts, and was frequently decorated with the American eagle to act as a reminder and celebration of America's newly won independence.

It was during this time that Mother Ann Lee started her first Shaker settlement near Albany, New York, having left Britain. Originally Quakers, the Shakers (so-called because of the paroxysms which seized the devotees during religious worship), believed in functionalism, and their growing number of communities were self-sufficient. Their simple design concept, that 'beauty rests on utility', produced inexpensive furniture with clean and elegant lines, often made from maple. Shaker furniture first became fashionable in 1860 and is enjoying a further revival during the 1980s and 1990s.

A revival of previous styles gripped Europe during the nineteenth century and its influence soon spread to America, where imitations of Renaissance, Elizabethan, Gothic, Rococo and oriental designs abounded. Other indigenous American furniture was also being produced, usually with the help of mass-production. By the 1880s the Arts and Crafts Movement was in full swing, and the British writer, Charles Eastlake, had a tremendous impact on the American branch of this revival, thanks to his book *Hints on Household Taste*, which demanded simplicity and good craftsmanship. Although many of the factories which copied the Eastlake style produced inferior work, some fine pieces were made, and Eastlake paved the way for such American Arts and Crafts designers as Stickley and Greene and Greene, both of whom were important in the development of Mission furniture.

This became popular in the 1890s and was based on the prevailing fashion for utility of design, which the exponents saw as their mission – hence the name. The furniture was simple and rectilinear, often made from oak and covered with leather, plain cloth or canvas.

An eclectic taste

Most houses today show a mixture of furniture styles, but wood usually predominates. In past years the High-Tech look created minimalist interiors that featured curved metal chairs, glass-topped tables and a bare, cool atmosphere. Inevitably, there has been a recent backlash against such modernism, with a huge revival in country and colonial furniture in particular. Pieces that would once have lingered at the backs of dealers' showrooms for months on end were suddenly reaching unheard-of prices, and the country folk who had always owned such furniture were amused to know they were now housing objects of value. Pine, one of the cheapest woods of all, is now highly

The furniture in this oak-beamed room is a mixture of styles, periods and woods, yet it combines to create a warm, comfortable atmosphere. The ornately carved cabinet is the focal point, but its exotic appearance is offset by plain shapes, such as the sofa and small oak table.

collectable, while mahogany, which enjoyed such popularity during the eighteenth and nineteenth centuries, is now an endangered wood and its use is not recommended unless there is a guarantee that the felled trees are being replaced with young saplings.

There is no doubt that fashions will continue to change, creating new ideas and movements, but the cabinet-makers, provincial craftsmen and designers of the past have left a magnificent legacy that will endure and be enjoyed for many generations to come.

THE
DIFFERENT
WOODS

Ash

According to John Evelyn, 'every prudent Lord of a Manor should employ one acre of ground with Ash to every twenty acres of other land, since in as many years it would be worth more than the land itself'. He may well have been right: not only is the wood flexible and strong, but it is also renowned for its curative and protective qualities – although not in a thunderstorm as ash trees are supposed to attract lightning – and was once a sacred tree that was worshipped. According to folklore, if you carry an 'even ash' – a leaf with an even number of matching leaflets – you will meet your lover before the day is over. Ash is reputed to ward off witchcraft, and to remove warts.

It is hardly surprising, then, that ash is traditionally the favoured wood for walking sticks – it's reassuring to know you've ventured outdoors with such a powerful good luck charm. The more prosaic qualities of ash also make it an important wood, and its ability to absorb shock has made it ideal when making such forms of transport as the skeletons of aeroplanes, early bone-shaker bicycles and the framework of Morgan sports cars. It is also used for sports equipment, such as tennis racquets, cricket stumps and hockey sticks, and for the handles of garden and striking tools.

Although its greyish-white colour makes ash very beautiful, it is best for furniture when given a stained finish, otherwise the wide grain can collect dirt. It responds exceptionally well to steam bending, and so is especially popular for ladder-back steam-bent chairs.

The ability of ash to absorb shock without splitting makes it ideal for sports equipment and the handles of garden and woodworking tools. In this photograph are a basket of ash logs; an old cart wheel; a carved wooden bowl which has been stained to enhance the grain; a croquet mallet; and various gardening tools, including spades and a scythe.

Beech

One of the most glorious trees of all, beech now rivals oak as the most commonly used hardwood, yet it has sometimes been overlooked in the past. When Julius Caesar visited Britain, on two occasions, he observed that there were no beech trees – erroneously, as it turned out. Folklore, usually so informative, remains strangely silent on the subject of beech trees, yet today beech is highly valued for its hard-working qualities.

Although beech dries easily, it can also become distorted. Even when it is dry, it can still move if there is a noticeable change in the humidity of the air around it. On the other hand, beech wood is strong, is a good choice for turning and has an attractive white or pale brown colour. Its close grain and good structure mean it is highly valued for making the handles and bodies of craftsmen's tools, as well as more mundane articles such as wooden spoons and other kitchen utensils. It is also one of the traditional woods used for whittling treen.

Beech is unsuitable for outdoor use, unless it has been treated with a good preservative, because it also rots easily. However it excels in the manufacture of cheap furniture. During the seventeenth century it was suitably stained and polished to act as a poor man's walnut or mahogany, but it came into its own during the development of bentwood furniture. Like ash (which is a more expensive wood), beech responds marvellously to bending and steaming, so was the prime wood for bentwood chairs, rocking chairs, hat stands and other curved designs.

The close grain and texture of beech makes it invaluable for utensils that will take a lot of wear. It is also an excellent wood for steam bending. In this photograph are a steamed hat box; kitchen utensils; a bread board; old-fashioned clothes pegs; old woodworking tools; an antique plane; hand-carved ladles; and a milking stool.

Cherrywood

In common with the other fruitwoods, cherrywood has always been a very popular timber for local craftsmen looking for a cheap source of material. Whenever they ran short of wood they could lop off a branch or two, or even fell a whole tree, and any useless offcuts would make aromatic firewood.

The main drawback of cherrywood, like the other fruitwoods, is that the trees don't grow very tall, although cherry is the largest of the lot. European cherry is a modestly sized tree, but its cousin, the American black cherry, can grow up to 90 feet (30 metres) tall. As a result, its use is limited to decorative work in furniture and cabinet-making, and it is one of the woods traditionally used for treen because it can be worked just as well by hand as by machine tools. Cherrywood is susceptible to decay, so is not recommended for use outdoors or in damp conditions.

Cherrywood will distort unless it is dried well, but it is quite stable after that, although it is not very stiff. It is pale pinky-brown when first cut, but exposure to the air soon darkens it, so that old pieces of cherrywood can almost reach the colour of mahogany. The limited size and availability of European cherrywood mean its use is mostly confined to special pieces of furniture, but American black cherry is more readily available. It is used for furniture, panelling and high-class joinery, and is also renowned as one of the favoured woods of traditional Shaker furniture although maple was used most often.

Although the short height and width of cherry trees means there is a limited supply of their wood, its size restrictions are far outweighed by its glorious colour and grain. The wood has always been popular with amateur craftsmen looking for a ready supply of material. This photograph shows a spice jar and an assortment of small boxes.

Elm

Thirty years ago the European landscape was full of stately elm trees, dark green in summer, yellow in the autumn and dark brown in the winter. Then, in the late 1960s, a particularly vicious strain of Dutch elm disease arrived in Europe from Canada, and swiftly spelt the end of tens of thousands of trees.

Until then, elm, oak and ash were the three great woods, especially in the days before steel. Elm is particularly valued for its structural qualities which endure even when the wood is permanently wet, so is chosen for fishing boats and barges. It was the Romans who first discovered this quality, so they built the first London Bridge on piles of elm. The Rialto in Venice is also built in this way, and ancient underground water pipes, many of which survive today, were usually made of bored-out lengths of elm. Open-air water pumps were also made of elm as the wood in the well did not rot and the wood above ground did not split when the water froze. Such sturdy qualities make it the natural choice for coffins and also for weatherboarding on the exterior of buildings.

Its interesting grain and pale brown colour makes elm a favourite with craftsmen, especially when they find pieces with very curvy grain. Because it resists pressure, elm was frequently made into floorboards in old buildings, especially if the owners couldn't afford oak, which was more expensive. It does not split either, so is a good choice for butchers' blocks, but one of its most famous uses is for the seats of Windsor chairs.

Elm is often used for weatherboarding because of its resistance to water, and it was used to build the large chicken coop shown in this photograph. In the foreground are a set of shelves with drawers below; a lyre-backed chair; a simple stool; a wheel with elm spokes; and an ancient mallet.

Oak

Throughout Europe, the mighty oak has always been regarded as a special, sacred tree. It symbolizes strength, presumably because it grows to such vast proportions, and the ancient Celts believed it was the tree of Thor, god of thunder, because it attracted lightning. Interestingly enough, research has proved that the oak tree is struck by lightning more often than any other. Objects made from a blasted oak were used as protective amulets. The tree is also home to mistletoe, a parasitic plant that the Druids considered sacred because of its host tree. Many place names incorporate the word oak somehow or other, which illustrates the symbolism of the tree down the ages.

The strength and durability of oak ensured it was the prime building timber for centuries. Historic buildings throughout the northern hemisphere are continuing examples of oak's reliability and versatility, especially classic half-timbered medieval buildings. The best oak timber comes from forest trees, as they grow tall and fast, producing wood that is both straight and strong.

Oak has played an important role in boat-building, especially in the British Royal Navy between the sixteenth and nineteenth centuries. It is also a fine wood for furniture and domestic flooring, and enjoyed a monopoly over all other woods until the advent of walnut and mahogany in the sixteenth century. Oak barrels are highly prized when making wines and spirits, as the tannic acid they contain imparts a distinctive flavour resembling vanilla.

There is something very reassuring about oak. It is partly due to its handsome grain and colour and its strength, but perhaps also because the houses and furniture made from it in the Middle Ages are still seen today. Shown here are two tall candlesticks; a chest; a large old lock; a butter churn; a cake stand; a huge drop-leafed table; a bread board; and a chair.

Pine

This is the most commonly used softwood of all, and over the past few years it has enjoyed a tremendous revival of popularity and interest. Many different varieties make up the pine family, with each tree growing in a particular area of the world. Yellow pine, radiata pine, pitch pine, ponderosa pine and western white pine are some of the most commonly grown trees, mostly in North America, South Africa and eastern Australia and New Zealand. Redwood, or Scots pine, grows throughout northern Europe as far as Siberia. The by-products of all these trees – turpentine, resin, pitch and tar – are as highly valued and important as the wood itself.

Pitch pine enjoyed a heyday in nineteenth-century America, when it was used to make furniture for churches, chapels and schools, plus more industrial uses. Its strength (it is much heavier than European redwood) makes it suitable for structural use and heavy construction work, while lower grades of timber are turned into crates, flooring and joinery. The wood is high in resin, which is a prime ingredient of turpentine.

Low-quality radiata pine is used to make crates, pallets, broom handles and flooring, while the better quality timber is used for furniture. It is an important pulpwood and its use is increasing rapidly. Sculptures and carvings are often worked from high-quality yellow pine, and it is also used for expensive furniture, cabinet-making, boat construction and some parts of stringed instruments.

Old country furniture was often made from pine, because the trees grew quickly and the wood was cheap to produce. Very cheap furniture was made from a mixture of pines and then painted. Shown here are some decoy ducks; a painted wheelbarrow; a birdcage; a small bedside cabinet; a painted stool; a stepladder and an old coal bucket.

Yew

The yew tree was once sacred to Hecate, goddess of the underworld, and throughout the succeeding centuries it has always borne a grim association with death. Churchyards often boast at least one yew tree (for which a remarkable age is usually justifiably claimed – up to 800 years), whose dark-leaved branches spread out over the crumbling gravestones and whose knobbly roots sometimes threaten to trip you up as you pass. Opinion seems divided about why a churchyard is the traditional home of the yew. Some old authorities claim it is because the yew is said to ward off devils (which is why yew hedges were frequently planted near houses), while others believed it was due to yew's ability to absorb the noxious smells that floated up from the graves.

The short, deeply fluted trunk of the yew tree rather limits its use. It is difficult and expensive to convert it into straight planks, so it is most frequently made into small objects such as pill and snuff boxes, and treen, or sliced into veneers for panelling. Yew was traditionally used for the bent parts of Windsor chairs because it responds so well to steaming. The most famous application of all, however, is due to the wood's elasticity and dates back hundreds of years to the English longbow. It's rather ironic that the home-grown archers who fired these massive weapons were specially chosen for their tremendous strength, but their bows were made from Spanish yew, which grew straighter than the curvy English variety.

One of the most famous products of the yew is the longbow, as shown here with a quiver full of arrows. The wood of the yew is often gnarled and knotty, so it is very unusual to find enough to make a self-bow, which is made from a single piece of yew. Yew is easily steamed, so when bent is a prime component of Windsor chairs.

Decorative Techniques

So-called country furniture has always been relatively simple, with its design dictated by such considerations as price, practicality and size. People on low incomes couldn't afford to buy anything ornate or elaborate; while if they made their furniture themselves they wouldn't have much time to spare for adding such decorative finishes as veneers, marquetry and inlays.

It was a different story, however, for the aristocracy and wealthy middle classes, especially during the period from the Renaissance to the early nineteenth century. Practical considerations were very low on their list of requirements when buying furniture, and instead they saw the pieces as reflections of their own knowledge and taste. This was especially so during the Renaissance, when fine interiors were regarded as a reflection of the owner's wisdom and erudition. As the years progressed, furniture assumed the same roles as painting and sculpture in a grand house. In fact, some of the most highly decorated pieces do look quite uncomfortable, and were obviously intended more to be admired than used.

Veneering and inlay are the two main decorative techniques, but inlay is further divided into marquetry, parquetry and Tunbridge ware. All these techniques have been popular at different times, but together they show the remarkable versatility and beauty of wood, and are a testament to the magnificent art of the cabinet-maker.

Veneering

Of all the techniques, veneering is the oldest and dates back to pre-Egyptian times. A thin layer of an attractively figured wood is glued on to an underlying layer of less expensive material. It is not only an economical use of expensive wood but it also gives extra strength to the whole piece, especially if the grain of the veneer is placed at right angles to that of the wood beneath.

Different methods of cutting sheets of veneer from a

Above: An example of marquetry showing an oyster veneer, from the late seventeenth century. At this time the art of marquetry was at its zenith, and some pieces were so elaborate they ranked as works of art with paintings and sculpture. **Right:** This is a detail of ivory inlay on ebony, from a secretaire made by Chippendale between 1770 and 1773.

log produce different sorts of figuring. For example, slicing horizontally across the tree trunk reveals the concentric rings of growth, while a striped grain is obtained by cutting the log in half lengthways. When the log (usually of bird's-eye maple) is rotated on a lathe, a continuous sheet of veneer is cut, rather like unwinding a swiss roll, producing a highly variegated pattern. The part of the tree from which the log comes will also affect the figuring: burr veneer is the most highly prized and is cut from the end grain of the irregular outgrowths that appear on many hardwood trees, including oak, elm, ash and walnut. Curl veneer is cut from the point where the main trunk meets a branch, and oyster veneer, which originated in seventeenth-century Holland, is made up of several sheets cut across the width of a small branch, usually walnut or laburnum.

Veneering was very popular with the Romans,

A William and Mary oyster-veneered laburnum chest, banded with fruitwood. The moulded top has been inlaid in a lobed pattern.

whose love of opulent decoration was reflected in their intricate inlay work using woods, precious metals and ivory, but it then disappeared in Europe until its revival during the sixteenth century with intarsia work, made up of many small pieces of veneer. Veneer has also been widely used for English and American furniture since the middle of the seventeenth century, and also in India, where ivory veneers acted as a protection against wood-boring and wood-eating insects.

Inlay

In this technique, various contrasting woods are recessed into a piece of solid wood to form patterns or even pictures, but the degree of detail is limited because the recesses must be cut out with gouges. The art of

inlay developed in Italy and southern Europe during the Middle Ages, but really came into its own with intarsia in fourteenth-century Italy. The *intarsiatori*, as the Italian craftsmen were called, were so skilled at inlay that it can be difficult to tell the difference between their work and perspective painting. Siena Cathedral contains excellent examples of the heights of perfection which intarsia reached, and many sixteenth-century Italian monasteries and palaces feature rooms panelled with intarsia, most commonly depicting landscapes, animals, still lifes and *trompe l'oeil*.

Early inlay mostly used simple contrasts between light and dark woods, but by the end of the fifteenth century the choice of woods had been broadened by the discovery that they could be stained, or even blackened with a hot iron.

Furniture featuring inlays often has, in addition, bands and strings, which are strips of inlay used to ornament and define the edges of large pieces of

A typical piece of Tunbridge-ware – a box decorated with a butterfly. Decorated boxes were a particular favourite of these craftsmen.

furniture such as cabinets, tables and desks. Herring-bone bands were another popular form of inlay, where two layers of wood veneers are arranged so the direction of their grains meet at an acute angle.

Marquetry

Another form of veneer inlay, marquetry was introduced into Britain from Europe during the Restoration in the mid-seventeenth century. Unlike inlay, the entire decorative area is cut out of different woods, using a very fine-bladed saw, so there is much more scope for creating tiny and intricate patterns. After being cut out with the saw (called a donkey), the individual pieces are glued, arranged on an underlying wood and clamped in place until the glue has set firmly. The woods used include mahogany, olive, boxwood, palisander, walnut and rosewood.

Brightly coloured floral marquetry was highly fashionable during the late seventeenth century in England and Holland, although these colours had been toned down considerably by the beginning of the eighteenth century. Much sixteenth-century German furniture is distinguished by its very elaborate marquetry, incorporating such decorative devices as strap work, birds and beasts; and French seventeenth-century furniture almost glitters with beautiful marquetry.

Parquetry

Strictly speaking, parquetry – pieces of geometrically-shaped veneer – is applied to floors, but it has also been used to decorate furniture as a form of marquetry. Whether on floors or furniture, it is characterized by its regular, repeating pattern of geometric shapes which

This commode is decorated with parquetry designs that accentuate the shape and curvature of the piece.

are often arranged to create a three-dimensional effect.

Strips of the woods to be used are arranged side by side, then cross cut so the resulting blocks can be slid up and down to create the patterns, although this is not practical for flooring where the pattern is built up by hand from individual blocks.

Some notable examples of parquetry include French and German furniture of the eighteenth century.

Tunbridge-ware

A form of wood mosaic that became popular in the English town of Tunbridge Wells during the nineteenth century. Unlike other mosaics, Tunbridge-ware is made from tiny strips of wood that are glued together into the finished pattern and then sliced into sheets of veneer, used to decorate little boxes, tables and desks.

LIVING WITH WOOD

Wooden Furniture

Since man first decided he

needed furniture he has made it

from wood: oak, ash, fruitwoods

and pines. Although the styles

and shapes have changed over

the centuries according to the

dictates of fashion and

circumstance, the beautiful

grains, textures and colours of

the woods have remained the

same, and the soft sheen of an

old piece of wooden furniture is

incomparable.

Chairs

Sitting on a chair was the prerogative of the nobility and senior clergy until the sixteenth century: ordinary mortals had to make do with stools and benches. That is how the phrase 'taking the chair' originated – you could only do so if you were important.

As the century progressed, stools began to develop back rests, but they were called 'backstools' so as not to cause offence to those who considered reclining in chairs to be part of their birthright. By the eighteenth century, the demand for chairs had increased dramatically and provided a thriving industry for anyone who lived near woodland (and therefore had a ready supply of the raw material to hand).

Those backstools were the predecessors of the popular Windsor chair, which was the first style to appear in cottages. It varied enormously in style and construction according to the region in which it was made, with seats made from elm or oak, legs of fruitwood, beech or birch and hooped backs of steam-bent yew.

Today, Windsor chairs are still evocative of simple country living, but there are many other styles of chair that are also suitable. A good hunt around a few antique or junk shops should reveal all manner of interesting chairs, with turned backs, rush or wicker seats or carved handles and arm rests. Some chairs look good stripped but others, because they were made from a variety of woods can resemble a wooden jigsaw puzzle when viewed in their natural state, and are best painted a soft sea green or pale blue.

Chairs come in all shapes and sizes, from babies' high chairs (an idea that originated in northern Europe) to corner chairs with two backs so you can choose in which direction to sit. Children's chairs are becoming increasingly collectable, and their diminutive size means they can be tucked away in corners or odd spaces where nothing else will fit.

Settles and settees

We may think that we live in the age of travel, but our medieval ancestors were also frequently on the move, which meant their furniture had to be portable too. Benches and stools could be easily moved from one place to another, but the settle was a result of the more stable life enjoyed by the middle classes towards the end of the Middle Ages. Essentially, a settle is a bench with a back panel and arms or side panels. However, the back was not just something to lean against: it also protected

the sitter from draughts (and there must have been plenty of them).

The design of settles barely changed between the seventeenth and nineteenth centuries, for the middle and upper classes had abandoned them in favour of settees and chairs, so they were a feature of servants' halls, cottages and other humble dwellings. Because storage space was at such a premium, the seats of settles often lifted up to provide a home for blankets and other household items, while better-quality pieces had cupboards built into the panelling around the base. Another style of settle, known as a monk's bench in Britain and a chair-table in America, had a back that folded down on to the arms to make a table.

Some settles even had cupboards fitted into their backs, and these could be used for anything from storing a side of bacon to hanging up coats. If you were very poor you might have slept in a bed settle, where the seat lifted out to form a big wooden box that was laid on the floor. Not exactly the height of comfort but at least the wooden sides would have acted as draught-excluders and provided a little warmth.

Settees were the natural successor to settles, as they had upholstered seats of leather or cloth and were therefore much more comfortable. They appeared in the seventeenth century and were succeeded by the less formal sofas. French furniture of the time was particularly exquisite, and the gilded *canapé* sofas and *bergères* exemplify the elegance of the period.

Above: The grace and charm of this Louis XV *canapé* sofa is unmistakable, with its scrolled back, carvings and curved legs. **Facing page:** In complete contrast is this lovely curved settle with panelled back. The cheerful cushions give it a comfortable seat and the curved back means that three or more people could sit in it at any one time and be able to see each other while talking, rather than have to peer over or round one another's heads. The battered paintwork adds to its charm and helps to create a sense of familiarity and ease.

Tables and desks

What would we do without tables? We sit around them to eat, work at them, decorate our homes with them and often cover them with miscellaneous objects. (Not so very long ago we even used to lay out our dead on them.) They range from small bedside tables with drawers and deep recesses for books and all the other paraphernalia without which one can't go to bed; side tables to put lamps or drinks on; occasional tables; folding and card tables that can be opened out when needed and then put away again; to their bigger relatives, refectory, kitchen and dining tables.

Originally, tables were very simply made from hardwoods (for durability), with straight sides and unadorned stretchers. But as the centuries progressed, such innovations as turned legs, folding flaps and removable sections appeared. Dining room tables were often very grand affairs, and the Georgians and Victorians excelled themselves when it came to producing beautiful French-polished tables made from such expensive woods as walnut.

The Georgians also loved nests of tables, which acted as side tables, but such items have no place in the country interior. Much nicer is a collection of small tables that has been amassed over the years, each one different but earning its keep through its beauty and individuality. Tables aren't usually left bare, so there is no need to despair if you have one with beautiful legs but a damaged top. You can always hide its deficiencies with a pretty tablecloth, piles of books, a drinks tray, bowl of fruit, collection of china or anything else that acts as good camouflage.

Desks, especially when they open up to reveal lots of tiny drawers and pigeon holes, look as though they're full of secrets. Some of the slant-topped desks that are sold in antique shops were once clerks' desks or even used in schoolrooms, and so may be decorated with a few ink blots (see Part 3, Caring for Wood, on how to remove them) and other evidence of wear and tear.

Facing page: Shaker furniture is instantly recognizable, with its clean lines and simplicity of style. This Bible box placed on top of a typical Shaker drop-leaf table can be found in the Deacon's Office of the Hancock Community, Massachusetts. The swivel chair's back is made from maple and the seat and legs from hickory. **Above:** This stained oak gate-leg table has barley-sugar turned legs. The cushions on the chairs suggest that they aren't very comfortable, and nor do they match the table, but they show how the country look is made up from a mixture of styles and shapes.

Staircases and banisters

When people who lived before the fifteenth century wanted to go upstairs, they had to clamber up ladders. Ladders didn't take up much space and were easy to move about, but must have been quite perilous after too much mead or one too many flagons of ale.

It was only during the sixteenth century that someone hit on the bright idea of securing wide oak ladders – with solid blocks for treads – to the walls, and boxing in the open sides with simple panelling. As the century progressed, stairs developed and became more like the flights we know today, with carved newel posts, balustrades and moulded handrails. By the seventeenth century, stairs were developing again, and short flights of stairs with landings superseded the original long flights which had sharp bends whenever a change in direction was required. At the same time, stairs were often given extra decoration, such as carved panels that ran up the walls of the staircase, painted walls or heraldic beasts that were carved into the tops of the newel posts; and more and more were given pride of place in the house.

During the eighteenth century, the vogue for Palladian architecture called for a lighter, more delicate touch. Sometimes existing oak staircases from a previous century would be altered to fit in with the prevailing fashions and create the necessary sense of drama. During the nineteenth century, the all-pervading mahogany took over from oak as the chosen wood, and smooth oval handrails were a special feature of the time.

Even in the smaller terraced houses that were springing up everywhere the staircases were important focal points, often with features borrowed from the grand houses of the previous century, and dog-leg turns enabled architects to tuck staircases neatly into place, leading off hallways with mosaic tiled floors, leaded lights or bay windows to continue the importance that this part of the house had traditionally been given.

Above: The pale oak stairwell of this converted English gatehouse is so decorative and architectural that it needs no further adornment or embellishment at all. Looking upwards reveals a beautiful pattern of bare beams supporting the small turret. **Facing page:** This oak staircase is chalk to the other's cheese, of course, and has a very different style and atmosphere, yet it still fulfils its intended function of being the focal point of the house. The square newel posts have been decorated with carved scrolls and the Tudor rose in classic Jacobean style.

In typical country cottages, of course, the front door may lead straight into the sitting room and the staircase lead straight out of it, usually at a steep angle. (You often have to duck your head as well to avoid taking off the top of it like a boiled egg.) Such staircases are so tiny that sometimes there is barely enough room for a human body, let alone much decoration other than a few paintings or sketches hanging on the stairwell.

On the other hand, bigger stairwells can be decorated in all sorts of ways to attract the eye. The wall up which the stairs climb can become a marvellous display area for a collection of paintings, silhouettes, drawings, posters, framed memorabilia or even, if such should be your taste, cases of stuffed fish or exotic butterflies and moths. Beautiful Turkish kilims or Persian rugs also look wonderful displayed on a stairwell. If space is at a premium, the area underneath the stairs, if not already a cupboard, could be converted into a mini library or even a small study, complete with tiny desk, chair and plenty of good lighting.

Instead of using carpet, the stairs can be left bare and waxed or polished, provided they have been built from a hardwood. Stencilled designs can run up and down the sides of them; they can be painted; or the treads can be left unpainted (because of the wear they will get) and just the risers decorated instead.

Facing page: This imposing staircase sweeps through Calke Abbey in Derbyshire, dubbed 'the house that time forgot'. It was built at the beginning of the eighteenth century and is a fine example of the wide, straight staircases of the time. **Above:** Opening out a house by removing a floor and creating a minstrels' gallery completely alters the feel of a house, making it seem very spacious, although in practice most of a floor will have vanished. There will be little privacy, however, so such considerations must be made before any work begins.

Dressers

Over the past twenty years the sale in old pine dressers has known no bounds. No one was interested in them until about thirty years ago, when fashions changed and the ever-rising cost of eighteenth-century elm and oak dressers firmly removed them from the price bracket of most people. Now good pine dressers seem to be moving in the same direction, especially if they incorporate features such as rows of tiny spice drawers,

a clock or glass-fronted cupboards to keep dust off the shelves and their contents.

Originally, of course, dressers belonged in the kitchen, and were so capacious, with their large roomy cupboards, recesses, drawers, racks and various flat surfaces, that they were essential pieces of furniture. In cottages, especially, they acted as dressers and sideboards combined; the only other furniture the cottager needed was a table, chairs and something to cook on. It wasn't until the Arts and Crafts Movement in the late nineteenth century that dressers, bearing painted mottoes and decorated with cut-work shapes, moved from kitchens into dining rooms. They were very popular both in America and Europe and inspired Charles Rennie Mackintosh to design fitted dining rooms that incorporated dressers.

So great is their current popularity that you can buy pine dressers in all sorts of shops, all manner of conditions and for all sums of money. Make sure you know what you are buying: some dressers are sold as 'antique pine' when in fact they are fresh from the workshop. Actually, they have been made to an old pattern using old pieces of wood, so it is the pine itself that is antique (you hope), not the dresser. Very often you can buy a truly antique, or at least genuinely old, dresser for less money than you would pay for one where the glue is still drying, and you will usually have a much nicer piece of furniture to boot. You should also be careful when buying a painted dresser that you hope

Above: China was stored in the dresser, but where did perishable foodstuffs go? Special cupboards with ventilated doors were the solution in the days before refrigeration, and they still look good today. **Facing page:** You would need a large dining room or kitchen to take a dresser of this size, but what a wonderful dresser it is, with its painted panels and numerous shelves. The back of the dresser has been painted cream rather than green to throw the displayed china into relief and enable one to see it better.

to strip back to the wood. It may have been painted in the first place because it was made from a hotchpotch of different woods, and so will look like patchwork when revealed in its natural state.

A dresser is usually the focal point of a room, so it pays to decorate it accordingly. Jugs, wooden animals, trailing plants, tureens, teapots or anything else large enough to be viewed from afar can be ranged along the very top of it, though it is not very practical to install anything that will be used frequently up there. Dog-kennel dressers, which have large recesses at the front between the cupboards, were intended to take large soup tureens but they also look good holding wicker baskets, earthenware *marmites* or huge jugs.

If you picture a dresser in your mind you will no doubt visualize rows of shelves crammed with an assortment of wonderful china and other treasures: plates, cups, mugs, jugs and bowls all look marvellous, especially if they are part of a collection that has been amassed with loving care over the years. There is something rather formal and contrived about a dresser that bears only one pattern of china unless, of course, it is very beautiful and rare. A jumble of sizes and shapes, perhaps in just a few colours, looks much better. If the handles of cups, mugs and jugs are sound they can be suspended from the shelves on hooks, increasing the cluttered feel and providing even more interest. The edges of the shelves can also be decorated with strips of lace or pieces of lacy paper for a fussier look.

The top and bottom halves of dressers are detachable, so it is not uncommon to see one without the other. Here, a very simple two-door cupboard has been used as a dresser, with a tiny wall-hung cupboard providing the shelving for a collection of jugs. The small chest of drawers would have been made by an apprentice.

Doors

There is something intriguing about doors – you wonder where they will lead you and what lies behind them – and so the more interesting they are to look at the better. In cottages and very old houses the doors are frequently much shorter than they would be if made today, reflecting people's average height at the time: if you visit anywhere built during the Middle Ages you will be astonished at how often you have to duck to pass through a doorway.

Period doors add real character and interest to a building, but even so that doesn't seem to stop some people removing the original doors and replacing them with ones that are flat (no interesting panels or intricate mouldings to dust) or completely out of sympathy with the style and feel of the property. It can be very disheartening to move into a period house that has lost some of its original features like this, although luckily they can usually be replaced, albeit at a price.

Another problem can be not having the original door furniture. During the 1960s it was all the rage to cover panelled doors with sheets of hardboard and to replace the original brass handles, escutcheons and finger plates with ones made from brightly coloured plastic or bevelled glass. (A lot of fireplaces were ripped out or boxed in too, to make way for gas or electric fires.) Happily, it is now easy to buy decent reproductions of period door furniture (if you can't afford to buy the originals) that should restore your doors to their former glory, whether that means tracking down elegant

Georgian brass door knobs, brass filigree finger plates or rustic metal latches.

There are other adornments to consider too: kitchen and bathroom doors were often thronged with brass hooks (who wants plastic?) to provide extra hanging space, and many a small child can't go to sleep without first making sure that no one is hiding behind the lumpy dressing gown hanging on the bedroom door.

Above: Many cottage doors are simply made from pieces of tongue and grooving, and they look good whether left polished, or painted. **Facing page:** Farmhouse doors are often much more rough and ready, made from vertical planks of wood held together with horizontal bars. The rougher such doors are the better they look, especially if the passage of time has removed a few chunks and made the knots fall out to reveal tiny peepholes. They may not be very efficient draught excluders, but you can always edge your chair closer to the fire and toast your toes.

Kitchens

The heart of any country home is its kitchen, a warm, comforting room filled with large, solid furniture and aromatic with the smells of spices, herbs and freshly baked bread. There will be a large, well-scrubbed table, probably made of pine, that has seated generations of hungry eaters – as well as providing a sturdy working surface, somewhere to arrange flowers and also a comfortable arm rest when chatting over a cup of tea.

Of course you don't need to live in the country to evoke this sort of atmosphere – you can create your own country kitchen in a city apartment or town house just as effectively as in a cottage with roses growing around the door. It is such items as the flooring, wall tiles, lights and decorations that can create a country atmosphere: perhaps quarry tiles on the floor, white-painted wooden shelves full of blue and white china, a bread crock with its original bread board lid, earthenware pots crammed with wooden spoons, an old-fashioned set of scales, bunches of drying herbs and garden flowers, a large clock with a homely tick and row upon row of jars filled with pulses and pastas, jams, preserves, pickles and chutneys.

Modern fitted kitchens may be streamlined and efficient, but very often they don't have any soul and they always have to stay behind when it's time to move. An unfitted kitchen, on the other hand, where every piece is separate, can travel with its owners from house to house and be altered or added to whenever necessary, providing a sense of continuity and familiarity.

This is a typical warm and inviting country kitchen, with its long kitchen table, comfortable armchair and old Persian carpet to add a splash of colour. Another bold sweep of colour is provided by the green frieze that acts as a huge pelmet across the windows and its accompanying cupboards and spice drawers.

Bedrooms

Clambering into a comfortable bed each evening must be one of the best moments of the day, so it is important to be in a bedroom that's cosy, relaxing and restful. Old and much-loved chests of drawers that glow in the light of bedside lamps, wooden chairs with their dainty seats and painted blanket boxes that crouch at the end of the bed all help to create atmosphere and a sense of being at peace with the world.

Traditionally, English cottage bedrooms are tucked under the eaves of the house and so have dormer windows and sloping ceilings. Oak beams that have darkened with age and centuries of wood-smoke are often contrasted with uneven white or cream painted walls covered with paintings and mirrors. American Colonial bedrooms have a very different feel, being generally much more spacious and elegant, and decorated with beautiful quilts made to traditional patterns, samplers, hooked rugs and embroidered or stitched cushions and pillow slips. Mediterranean bedrooms that are flooded with sunlight can stand stronger, darker colours such as reds and blues, which might be nothing short of depressing or claustrophobic in bedrooms that never see the sun.

Ask most people what sort of bed they would most like to sleep in and the answer is likely to be a four-poster or canopy bed. These huge pieces of furniture, which almost look like ships in full sail when festooned with their proper hangings (plus canopies if they were British), are redolent of romance and history. The

These deep reds and blues could only work in a bedroom that received plenty of light and air, as otherwise they would be very sombre indeed. The ornate carving around the bedhead contrasts well with the simplicity of the antique American quilts and is echoed in the two chests that sit either side of the bed and act as bedside tables.

truth, of course, is somewhat different. In the past, beds were given thick hangings to shut out the fierce draughts that swirled around bedrooms and provide some privacy in rooms that were often full of people. The bed was the most important and expensive piece of furniture in the whole house because a host of rituals was associated with it: births, marriages, illnesses and deaths. Even so, the bed itself could be quite a simple affair because it was always hidden by swathes of fabric, so they were what cost the money. In the big medieval houses special hangings would be used for lying-in after giving birth and also for laying out the dead. The hierarchy of a house could be detected by who had a four-poster (the most important member); followed by those who had half-canopies or half-testers, where the hangings just protruded over the head of the bed. Servants often slept in their masters' or mistresses' rooms on press beds, which folded away into tall cupboards when not in use, or in their own quarters, on truckle beds, which were made of pine and fitted with wheels.

One of the classic ingredients of a country bedroom is a quilt, whether it has been passed down through the family over generations, recently made by hand or bought from a specialist shop. American quilts tend to be made in specific two-colour pictorial patterns, such as the basket design, while their British counterparts, which are known as patchwork quilts, use a wide variety of fabrics in pieced or mosaic patterns. Both need considerable care, especially if they are old.

The contrast in style between these two bedrooms is startling. **Facing page:** The Gothic splendour of the marvellous four-poster bed dominates this room, and has wisely been left to speak for itself. The neutral colours of the furnishings throw the dark oak into relief, and the white canopy reveals the intricate carvings in all their glory.
Above: 'Beauty rests on utility' according to the Shakers, as this bedroom in Harvard, Massachusetts, demonstrates. Everything in the room has a purpose and there are no unnecessary objects.

Chests and cupboards

Chests have always been essential pieces of furniture, swallowing up a vast collection of clothes, blankets, papers and other, often less decorative, household paraphernalia. In the past, chests also acted as safes, housing anything that the master or mistress thought might prove irresistible to light-fingered servants. Spices and other expensive foodstuffs, for example, were highly prized – and coveted, presumably – so they were always kept under lock and key by the housekeeper. Interestingly enough, this practice is continued today in many restaurant kitchens by head chefs.

Originally, chests contained lots of small boxes that were stacked on top of one another and loaded from the top. However, that was so inconvenient, because you had to unpack them all every time you wanted to get at anything, that the boxes at the bottom were soon placed in the lateral openings already cut into the base of the chests. In time, the lower boxes became sliding drawers in what were known as 'mule chests'. These were very popular in America and were used as blanket chests, usually made of pine because oak was hard to find and too heavy to carry about in those unsettled times. Very often these blanket chests were beautifully painted and decorated (usually in black and dull red) to relieve the plain appearance of the wood and make them look more attractive. They are real collectors' items today on both sides of the Atlantic, and deservedly so. In the meantime, the idea of top-loading chests had been discarded in favour of the chests of drawers we know today.

Cupboards are relatively new pieces of furniture which first appeared in medieval Europe and were usually made of oak. They were known as 'presses' and contained shelves to store linen and clothing. By the seventeenth century these presses had begun to evolve into more specialized cupboards, such as beautiful French armoires, ornate clothes presses and huge, often ugly, Victorian mahogany wardrobes.

Above: This English oak washstand has changed considerably since it was first used as an essential part of the day's *toilette*. Originally it probably had a thick marble top, and the basin and ewer would have lived in the cupboard when not in use. Towels and other linen were stored in the drawers, ready for use. **Facing page:** This is a modern seed or spice chest copied from an old Colonial design. It is made from pine stained dark brown and has twenty-five drawers, and its simple design and construction accurately reflect the needs of the time.

Panelling and beams

Strange but true: medieval oak beams are so coveted and desirable that you can now buy reproductions of them in wood or plastic and nail them to your ceiling to create your very own version of a half-timbered house. Quite apart from the fact that these beams can look completely false, they are also often installed in houses that belong to the wrong period or style, or made to run in the opposite direction to the floorboards when they should run parallel (the joists that support the floorboards should fit into them at right angles).

It is far better, if you want to introduce some character into an otherwise bland-looking room, to give it some form of panelling. You can lower a very high ceiling with panelling, panel the walls from top to bottom or extend panelling from a dado downwards. It is an excellent way to camouflage uneven or unattractive walls that would otherwise require messy replastering or considerable decorating ingenuity. The type of panelling you choose will, of course, be dictated by cost, logistics and availability, but it can range from very expensive but equally beautiful carved wooden panels from a supplier of architectural salvage to simple tongue and grooving bought from a local hardware store and painted yourself.

Above: The beams in this Welsh farmhouse form a dramatic pattern that is complemented by the simple white-painted walls; any other decoration would distract the eye and spoil the effect. **Facing page:** At the other end of the scale is this equally stunning room, with panelling that incorporates shelving, corner cupboards, drawers and even wine racks. The wooden columns that rise up either side of the fireplace have been painted to tie in with the painted plasterwork ceiling moulding.

Decorative Wood

As well as its many practical
uses, wood is also much sought
after for its decorative qualities.
Carpenters choose to work with
particular woods for their grain,
colour or texture, as well as
their durability. Some woods,
such as box and lime, are
excellent for carving, while
others, such as cherry, turn well
and so are ideal for making
bowls and objects with similarly
curved shapes that show off the
lovely grain.

Toys

We all grow up with toys and so frequently take them for granted, little realizing the history or tradition that is attached to so many of them. When we're children life is very simple – we either have a particular toy and enjoy playing with it or we long for one that we don't have and embark on a campaign to make our parents' lives a misery until it magically appears in a Christmas stocking or as a birthday present.

But even a brief glance at the history of toys reveals that things aren't really that simple. Toys and children have always been synonymous, and many of the toys played with today have very strong links with the past. For example, you might think that clever merchandising is a product of the twentieth century, but it dates back a lot further than that. Roman children no doubt pestered their parents to buy them one of the replicas of the Trojan horse that were sold at the ruins of Troy.

Even the dead were provided with toys: wooden balls were being placed in tombs as far back as 1400 BC. The children of Ancient Egypt played with painted wooden cows and horses and wooden hoops.

Until the eighteenth century wood was the most popular material for toy making because of its versatility, cheapness and wide availability. Parents who couldn't afford to buy toys for their children would whittle little dolls or other simple playthings out of wood from the local forest or piece of common land. If you were wealthy, however, the sky was the limit.

In the seventeenth century, Nuremberg in Germany

was the centre of the European toy-making industry, and was renowned for its dolls' houses and dolls' rooms. Dolls' kitchens were particularly popular, as they were designed to teach small girls the mysteries of good housekeeping. On the whole, though, dolls' houses at this time were so expensive and delicate they were intended more for ladies of leisure than their children. In seventeenth-century France, Madame de Maintenon had a most beautiful dolls' house when she was the mistress of Louis XIV, but after she became his queen and rather pious with it, she had it converted into a dreary penitent's closet.

Above: The front of this dolls' house is quite elaborate, with its dormer windows, central clock and balcony that runs the width of the first floor: the dolls who live in it must feel very privileged. **Facing page:** This dolls' house belonged to the late Lady Margaret Samuelson, who had the second largest collection of dolls' houses in Britain. Like all period dolls' houses it is an excellent study of the living conditions at the time it was made. Such furnishings as the wallpapers, carpets and curtains would have been woven or printed especially for use in dolls' houses.

If you were very rich, a lot of the furniture in your dolls' house would be made of silver, and what's more you would have valued it so highly that you'd have mentioned it in your will. The Dutch especially loved coaches, soldiers and horses made from silver, while the English preferred silver utensils. Even so, making the wooden furniture was a highly skilled job and one at which the carpenters of Nuremberg excelled so much that they were able to export their work.

By the eighteenth century, dolls' houses had become real works of art in their own right, but were still so expensive that only the rich could afford to buy them. And no wonder – such notable architects as Sheraton, Adam and Chippendale all made dolls' houses at one time or another. When Robert Adam was designing an English house called Nostell Priory in about 1733, a dolls' version of the house was made too. The house carpenter felt that making the furniture for it was

Above: This early American rocking horse has been given a full complement of equipment, from his bridle to his saddle and stirrups. His rather battered appearance suggests that his small owners were keen riders: there is nothing sadder than an antique toy in pristine condition, such as an old teddy bear that hasn't gone bald – it suggests that it's been unappreciated and unloved. **Facing page:** Too much love rather than too little has obviously been the problem for these dilapidated rocking horses, which are awaiting some urgent running repairs and careful restoration.

beneath him, so he gave that task to his apprentice, a promising young man called Thomas Chippendale.

Despite always being about twenty years behind the prevailing fashions, dolls' houses provide an accurate record of the way people, and not just dolls, lived. French dolls' houses were very sumptuous affairs indeed (imagine having a doll-sized version of Versailles) – until the Revolution, presumably, when such items would have been regarded as betrayals of noble birth. Early American dolls' houses accurately imitated the plain colonial style of the time.

The manufacture of dolls' houses was quite a going concern by the nineteenth century, and they were widely available at toy bazaars throughout Europe and America. They were much simpler than their forerunners and were often decorated with high-quality imitation rosewood furniture or even birchwood furniture that was exported from Russia. By the turn of the century, dolls' houses were still very popular but it seems even they were victims of the spate of new building – they frequently had thin walls and badly proportioned rooms. Since then, dolls' houses have continued to be very popular toys for children and adults alike, and can be bought in every conceivable style from Palladian mansions to *Dallas*-style ranches.

Hobby-horses have an equally long history, dating back to the Greeks. They also appear in medieval illustrations, including a French psalter of 1300 and a French Book of Hours.

Left: Children of a nervous disposition should beware of playing with some of these wooden toys. One of the joys of wood is that nimble-fingered parents with little money can whittle or carve toys out of it very cheaply, and the interesting anatomical conditions of some of these dolls certainly suggest that they've been made at home.

The other popular equine toy is, of course, the rocking horse. This really came into its own during the eighteenth century, when it was usually made of red cowhide and equipped with wheels. The balance of some of these early models often left something to be desired, and many anxious nurses must have watched their charges wobbling about. Originally, rocking horses went up and down on springs, just as you would on a real horse, and were made from stuffed leather with real horsehair tails and manes. It was only later, when their popularity grew and their price dropped accordingly, that they were made of varnished wood, which wasn't nearly so comfortable or comforting. They still had leather saddles and reins, of course, and in

Above: This wonderful selection of antique early American toys must have provided hours of fun. The small shops and rooms on the bottom row of shelves are relatives of the dolls' house. The baker's shop – the Real Good Bakery – in the photograph is fully equipped with all that a real good baker needs, except for clients, but perhaps they're busy in their own shops and dolls' rooms. This collection is so charming that it's no surprise many adults are even more devoted to dolls' houses and rooms than children.

America, they sometimes had tasselled net covers too. In Britain, their decoration was even affected by the rise of the Arts and Crafts Movement.

Antique rocking horses, hobby-horses and dolls' houses can all fetch high prices in today's market and are eagerly snapped up by collectors at prices that show just how popular old toys are. They make marvellous decorations in rooms and are sometimes far too precious to be used by children any more. Dolls' houses often take pride of place in sitting rooms where they are proudly displayed on tables or chests, and rocking horses can also look good in bedrooms, on landings or sitting in bay or bow windows, just waiting for someone to ride them once more.

Above: This is a collection of antique children's rocking chairs and push chairs from Castle Drogo in Devon, the remarkable house designed by Sir Edwin Lutyens around 1910. The rocking horse on the left with the round seat is a very early example and would have been particularly suitable for a toddler, who could hold on tight to the rail without toppling over – very old rocking horses were not noted for their balance and stability. The double rocking chair in the foreground operated on the same principle as the see-saw and must have been great fun to use.

Collections

If you've got it, flaunt it, so some people say, and it makes sense when showing off collections of prized objects. What use is there in spending years amassing a special collection if all it's going to do is moulder away in a cupboard where no one can see it?

The golden rule to remember when displaying a prized collection, is to keep everything together. That has a much more dramatic impact than splitting up your collection and dotting it about the house or jumbling it up with something else. Window-sills, mantelpieces, book shelves, kitchen dressers, side tables and other vantage points all make excellent display areas. Very

fragile objects may also benefit from being placed in a glass case (the top of a dresser which has glass-fronted doors would be ideal) and kept out of sunlight or away from strong sources of heat.

If you are thinking of starting up a collection from scratch, it's a very good idea to choose something that is neither highly fashionable (and therefore highly priced – unless of course money is no object) nor so unique as to be completely unavailable. Very often it's the unusual, different, collections that attract the most interest and are the greatest fun to build up, rather than those that are more popular. At the moment, for

Facing page: Anyone hungry? There are many examples of wooden fruit, some of which, it has to be said, look more convincing than others. Yew is particularly suitable because its interestingly curved grain is shown off to perfection.
Above: Boxwood is renowned as one of the best woods for reproducing images. If the endgrain of a block of boxwood is carved it will hold detail better than any other wood and reproduce up to a million impressions; it is far superior to metal blocks.

example, antique Shaker objects and original decoy ducks are at the height of fashion and therefore command correspondingly high prices, but is anybody collecting little woolly models of sheep?

It's rather ironic that many ordinary, household objects from the past are now highly collectable. Treen are kitchen implements that were whittled out of chunks of wood, usually by dextrous husbands for their wives, or besotted suitors for their loves. If you needed some new clothes pegs, for instance, you asked your husband nicely if he'd make you some. Many young men who were tongue-tied in the presence of their beloveds, or who simply enjoyed romantic gestures,

would turn their treen into love tokens which carried secret messages. A spoon with a heart signified love, or with spheres carved inside openwork cages showed the girl that her admirer's heart was held captive by her charms. Two objects linked together by a pair of spectacles meant 'I want to see you' (in some cases it probably also meant that love is blind).

Snuff boxes, bowls, platters, cups, ladles, chopping blocks, pestles and mortars and washing bats (used to whack the excess water out of the washing) are all described as treen. A variety of woods was used, according to whatever was nearest to hand, but such hardwoods as sycamore, oak and maple were the most

Facing page: There are two collections here – some Ifugao baskets and six turned English candlesticks.
Above: At first this collection of framed pictures looks as though it is a complete jumble, but close inspection reveals that the pictures have been arranged in a symmetrical pattern after all, but using a variety of frames to prevent the display becoming too formal.

popular. Birch, beech, laburnum, walnut, fruitwoods, holly, yew and box were also used. Strictly speaking, objects are not pure treen if they were made later than 1830, which is when machine-made objects were first produced, but they are still highly collectable.

Wooden tea caddies are another example of how household objects have broken free from their simple beginnings and become extremely covetable. In the days when tea was a very expensive commodity and had to be kept in a safe place, tea caddies were very sophisticated affairs and came complete with a lock and key. A good example of a Georgian tea caddy, for instance, is currently worth a great deal of money.

Wooden objects associated with smoking can form the basis of a good collection too, even if that does seem highly contentious in today's anti-smoking world. They are divided into six categories: pipes; pipe cases; tobacco jars; tobacco boxes; pipe trays, stands and racks; and tobacco stoppers. The pipes, pipe cases and pipe trays all vary in shape and size according to the type of pipe that was smoked at the time they were made. Plenty of wooden tobacco jars were made because wood was so cheap, and many are highly decorative and made from turned or ringed wood.

Gameboards made from painted wood look very decorative displayed on a wall. If you decide to collect them and are torn between buying a worn board and one that looks much fresher, then as a general rule you should choose the worn one – it's probably worth more.

Right: This collection of treen shows how different the pieces can be in both size and shape. Among the varied objects is a pear-shaped tea caddy made from fruitwood, a powder shaker for kid gloves and a pestle and mortar. The small flat round box contains a puzzle game, and two tall needle cases stand immediately behind it – the one on the left contains needles for fine cloth and the one on the right is for thicker needles for canvas.

Picture and mirror frames

It is astonishing the difference an imaginatively chosen frame will make to a painting, bringing out all sorts of colours and shades that you missed before, and even giving what was a rather pallid picture some definite character and interest. Shops that specialize in framing carry a wide range of wooden frames, many of which are highly decorative (and correspondingly expensive) and made from such woods as beech, maple, walnut, yew and limed oak. Pine is usually a much cheaper alternative which you can wax, stain, stencil or paint. If you are skilled in the art of paint techniques you could even lacquer or marble a simple wooden frame.

If you are on the look-out for old frames, one of the best hunting grounds is a junk or antique shop filled with discarded paintings. Very often the paintings themselves are hideous chocolate-box affairs, but the frames may be another matter – perhaps ornate and gilded or lovely carved wood. It doesn't much matter if, when you've got them home, the frames don't fit any of your existing paintings because you could easily have them turned into mirrors instead by a professional glazier. Highly gilded and ornate mirrors can look surprisingly good in bathrooms, as well as their more usual positions above mantelpieces or over sofas.

It is important to choose picture or mirror frames that match their settings. **Above:** The collection of small, rather delicate, picture frames in this English cottage are set against a plain white wall to show them to their best advantage. **Facing page:** A very different style is shown in this Philadelphia room, where the dark, sombre colours of the naïve nineteenth-century painting are echoed in the painted blanket chest from an earlier period. The painting has been given a plain black frame – anything else would look out of keeping.

Carvings

Mention wooden carvings to most people and sooner or later the name of Grinling Gibbons will come up. Regarded by many as the master of wood-carving, Gibbons was born in the Netherlands in 1648, but was discovered in Deptford, London, in 1671 by John Evelyn, who introduced him to Sir Christopher Wren and Charles II, with sublime results that are still visible today. Gibbons' naturalistic style of carving exercised such an influence over his contemporaries that imitations of his work can be seen all over the world.

Like many of the medieval woodcarvers, Gibbons' favourite wood for carving was lime because it is so easy to work and has such a wonderful creamy colour. However it is not very strong and is delicious to woodworm, so it's not surprising Wren insisted that the carved wood in St Paul's Cathedral should be seasoned oak instead because it would last much longer.

Gothic and Romanesque architecture served as the inspiration for carvers of the Middle Ages, but by the sixteenth century the influence of the Italian Renaissance was being felt across Europe. As a result, the carvings featured a blend of cupids, acanthus leaves and similarly classical ornamentation with the more usual Gothic images. As fashions changed and the more formal, controlled Palladian style took over, so furniture and house interiors became much plainer.

In the ancient courts of Egypt, India and Persia, ebony was the most highly prized wood for carving. In medieval Egypt, where wood was very scarce and

had to be imported (mostly pine and oak from Turkey), small panels were carved with great intricacy and then joined together. Not only did this mean every scrap of wood could be used, but that the furniture was able to expand and contract in the hot days and cold nights without warping or splitting.

Above: Rounded shapes are the easiest to carve, such as these seed heads and rose hips, and in the past carvers would work on pieces they could execute with confidence. For example, such objects as shells, birds, fish, musical instruments and medals required considerably more skill than such fruits as oranges, lemons and pomegranates.
Facing page: This beautiful cherub definitely comes into the first category of highly skilled work. The bevel of the carving tool that was used would have given the wood a natural burnish.

Working Wood

Clothes horses, walking sticks,

umbrellas, musical instruments,

cricket bats, tennis racquets,

hairbrushes . . . All sorts of

everyday items are made from

wood, and they often deserve

greater interest. In some cases

the traditions remain unchanged

over the centuries, while in

others new techniques and skills

have been adopted, but wood

has remained one of our most

valuable and versatile resources.

Walking sticks and umbrellas

Not so long ago, no self-respecting gentleman would leave home without his walking stick, cane or umbrella, regardless of the weather.

Canes are very thin, usually made from malacca (a smooth bamboo with a mottled surface) and have always been carried more for dress purposes than practical ones. Walking sticks and umbrellas, on the other hand, must be strong enough when leant on to bear the weight of the person carrying them, so are made from a rich variety of hardwoods.

You might think that one umbrella is much like another, but to the trained eye of an expert a person's choice of umbrella (and the width of its shank – narrow is considered classiest) speaks volumes about his or her social position, aspirations, profession and personal style. For instance, chestnut is lightweight and gives a broad handle, so is preferred by people who can't grip very well and need something solid to lean on. Hickory is the strongest wood and most traditional, so is chosen by sticklers for convention. The beautiful grey-blue colour of ash resembles a piece of marble, and so would appeal to some and horrify others. The classic choice of the Victorians and Edwardians was a malacca handle (each piece of malacca is differently mottled and so is easily recognized by its owner) and a birch shank. In the 1920s whangee handles (a rougher, very knobbly type of Japanese bamboo) were preferred. Today, the choice is yours.

Walking sticks have always inspired imaginative craftsmen to turn a shaft of wood into anything from a real work of art to a complete flight of fancy. Craftsmen often carve handles into the heads of animals, birds or humans, or snakes may entwine themselves down the shanks. Little wonder they form such fascinating collections.

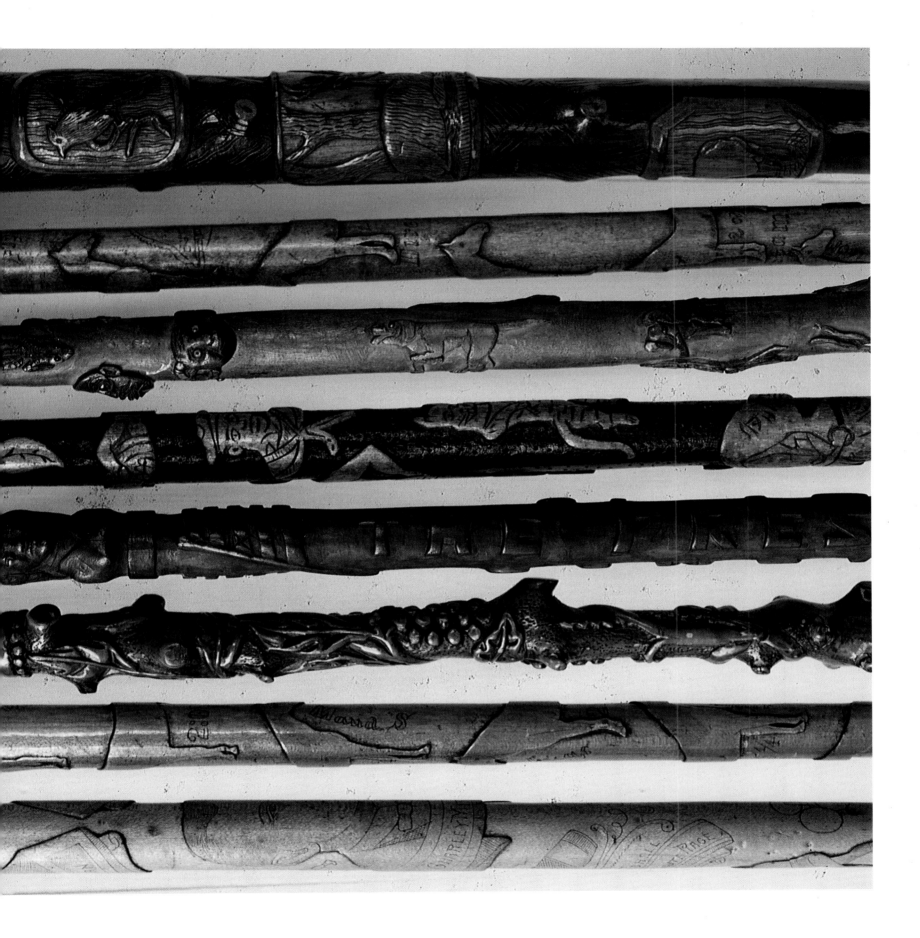

Tools of the trade

Wine has been aged in wooden barrels since Roman times, and today it is considered a sign of a good wine if it has been matured in young oak casks. The magical combination of oak and oxygen produces extra tannin and vanillin, which gives the wine a characteristic vanilla flavour. However, wine-makers don't just use any old oak for their barrels – the region in which the oak was grown is considered to be very important. For instance, when Californian Chardonnay is aged in barrels of French oak, it tastes very similar to the white burgundy that is usually matured in them. Some wine buffs tie themselves in knots arguing the case for different oaks for different wines. They claim to be able to taste the difference, and no doubt spend many happy hours practising to make absolutely sure. The tannic acid present in oak, which is so useful when maturing wine, is also used to cure leather skins and hides – hence the name, tanning.

Many tools have centuries of tradition behind them. Some specialist tools are easily recognizable, while others are quite mystifying unless their use is explained. The link between most, however, is that they will have been made of beech, especially if they are old. The close grain and excellent structure of beech has always made it a highly popular choice for handles, as has elm, which is one of the strongest woods of all.

Above: These oak wine vats come from the cellars at Mas de Dame in Provence. New oak barrels lose the full impact of their flavour after a couple of years, but the insides of the barrels can be shaved away, removing their lining of tartrate crystals at the same time, to reveal fresh wood. **Facing page:** An example of specialist tools is seen in this harness shop in Williamsburg, Virginia. The beech handles and heads are clearly visible.

Kitchen utensils

Look around the kitchen department of a supermarket or department store today and you will be nearly dazzled by a shining array of stainless steel, aluminium and glass. You might almost think you were buying equipment for an operating theatre, not a kitchen.

Advocates of country kitchens don't have to throw away all their labour-saving devices, electrical appliances and the very latest gadgets, but they can modify them with a few judiciously placed reminders of days gone by, or even hide the modern appliances behind cupboard doors and leave the old utensils on display. Bread crocks that stand on the floor and have bread board lids can still be found, as can wooden platters, egg racks, old-fashioned trays, butter pats, rolling pins, coffee mills, cheese boards and cutlery trays. An old-fashioned wooden draining rack can be

Above: The Shaker ideologies of neatness and tidiness applied particularly in their kitchens, which one can imagine sparkled like new pins. Kitchen implements would have been hung from the ubiquitous peg rails when not in use, as these shovels seen here in the Hancock Community, Massachusetts. The beautiful bowl would have been turned from a single piece of maple, chosen because it has no smell and therefore doesn't taint food.

fitted above the sink to house crockery that's used every day and a roomy plate rack makes a good display unit for favourite plates and dishes.

Some antique wooden kitchen utensils, such as tiny spice drawers, can fulfil their original function and also look decorative, while others, such as rolling pins, ancient wooden spoons and meat tenderizers, are best used for display purposes only in a stone crock, enamel flour bin or large Kilner jar.

If trips around antique shops don't reveal the old tray, bowl or cutlery box you are looking for you might prefer to buy a new one and give it a suitably distressed finish yourself. You can round off any perfectly square-cut edges with some fine sandpaper, paint the object and then immediately remove most of the wet paint with a cloth or even leave it in the garden for a while to let the sun and rain do their work.

Wicker baskets also look good in kitchens, whether they are suspended on hooks from the ceiling, sit on top of kitchen cabinets or tuck into the recesses of dressers. You can use them for anything from large bread or fruit baskets to containers for dried flowers or colourful glossy vegetables such as aubergines (egg-plants), courgettes (zucchini), and peppers.

Above left: Much too precious to be used now, such lovely old moulds as these were once treasured utensils. The round moulds could be used as stamps on butter or gingerbread biscuits, and the wonderful textured rolling pins were used to imprint patterns on shortbread dough. **Above right:** This is a collection of antique cutlery trays, behind which sit a variety of chopping boards. The cutlery trays were given handles so they could be carried to the dining table and then back to the kitchen. A display like this would look marvellous on a kitchen wall.

Gardening tools

Good, solid hardwoods such as ash, beech and elm have always been chosen to make the handles of garden tools because they are very strong and will only split under extreme strain. Their varnish may wear off over the years, leaving the exposed wood to become bleached and smoothed through constant use, but that only adds to their attraction.

Man has made his own gardening tools ever since he first began to cultivate his own fruit and vegetables, and the design of many of them has barely changed over the centuries. The earliest known form of wheelbarrow, for example, was in existence long before the Middle Ages. Known as a handbarrow, it must have been hard work for the two gardeners who had to carry it, stretcher-like, around the garden, for it had no wheels and must have weighed a great deal when carrying a full load of garden refuse destined for the compost heap. After that came early wheelbarrows which were made entirely of wood, with the exception of the iron rings that enclosed the simple wheels and therefore stopped them becoming pitted, splintered or worn out. Variations on the basic wheelbarrow design included barrows with detachable sides that could be added to increase their carrying capacity and thus save time in the garden. Such old wheelbarrows are now much sought after, but because they are too precious to wheel about any more they are frequently planted up like huge containers and used as decorative features.

Trowels and hand forks are very old designs, as are scythes and sickles, although using them correctly (when they can be just as effective as a lawnmower) seems to be a dying art. Hay forks and rakes were once made entirely from wood, steamed into shape, and simple besom brooms, made from bundles of twigs bound to a long straight pole, were essential for sweeping in and outside the house.

Above: These garden tools have obviously seen years of steady service, although it must have been quite difficult to use the three-pronged fork and the wooden spade effectively. **Facing page:** Some garden tools that are universally popular today were originally only known in a small region, such as these Sussex trugs, which were once used to carry coal or wood as well as garden produce. The baskets are made from willow and the main frames and handles from steamed strips of chestnut nailed into place.

Clocks

The steady tick of a much-loved clock is a classic ingredient of a comfortable home. You can buy a wide variety of clocks in antique shops but, according to the price you pay, you might have to take a pinch of salt with you, ready for any fervent assurances that the clock works as well as any modern counterpart. The problem is that many old clocks were made entirely of wood, which was easy to cut into the required pieces to make the movements, but is not as reliable as the more expensive metal. Wood also created more friction than metal, but the only lubricant of the time was animal fat, which soon became very sticky and must also have stunk to high heaven after a short while in a warm room. The answer was to use lignum vitae for the working parts, as it has a naturally oily surface and so lubricates itself.

Wooden clocks were among the first objects to be mass-produced: in America, one Connecticut manufacturer made 4000 wooden clocks between 1807 and 1810. Shakers, however, were still making their clocks by hand in the nineteenth century to their clean-lined designs. With the obvious exception of their long-case clocks, all other clocks would be carried from room to room as required and suspended from the peg rails that ran around the walls, and every community had its own single alarm clock.

Above: This wonderful curved Swedish clock has been made from three separate woods, each one chosen for its particular colour and grain. It needs no further embellishment and dominates this sophisticated interior, despite being curiously at variance with the elegant pier tables and sombre oil paintings. **Facing page:** This huge clock also dominates its surroundings, yet it blends in marvellously with the overall feel of the room, and especially with the dark oak beams.

The specialist woods

Thousands of species of timber are known in the world, but it is surprising how difficult it can be to find woods with the right combination of properties for particular needs. When it comes to finding woods that offer strength but resilience and flexibility too, the choice is very limited indeed.

Ash and hickory are the two time-honoured woods chosen for sports equipment, for example, because both are able to absorb shock without transmitting it to the player's arm, and they will stand continual impact without fracturing. Ash is the favoured wood for baseball bats: when the bat hits the ball, the heavy mass and weight of ash give the ball its speed and momentum. The heads of hockey sticks are also made of ash, steam-bent into a tight curve, with a cane handle to absorb shock. Modern skis are often made from laminated hickory, but ash is the traditional wood, and was once used in solid pieces.

Many world-class tennis players are now choosing man-made materials for their racquets, but ash has been the traditional wood since the game was invented. Originally the racquets were made of solid ash and so weighed a hefty 1 lb (450 g) or more – no wonder photographs of Victorian and Edwardian players show them looking so tired. Lamination arrived in the 1930s and allowed today's featherweight racquets, which usually have seven or eight laminations.

Lignum vitae is the traditional wood for bowls, although a shortage has meant that many bowls are

It must have been the greatest fun to dash down snow-covered hills and slopes on one of these lovely old sledges. Ash is the best wood to use when making them as it has its own inbuilt suspension, but its beautiful grey grain has been hidden here by bright paint, cheerful patterns and such swift-sounding names as 'Hustler' and 'Hornet'.

now made from composition materials. Bowls are made in sets of four from a single log, and no two sets are ever quite the same, so the player must become familiar with the characteristics of his particular set.

Completely different characteristics are needed for musical instruments, which require woods with considerable resonance. Spruce is highly valued for this reason, and is widely used to make the soundboards of pianos and other keyboard instruments, plus the bellies of violins, lutes, guitars and other stringed instruments. Lime is used for harps, while East Indian ebony is used for the black piano keys, and the finger boards, tail pieces and saddles of stringed instruments.

Sycamore is another traditional choice for these instruments, especially high-quality violins. The trees that will be used are chosen with great care and may be up to one hundred years old when they are felled. To make the back, logs are cut into radial wedges which are then invisibly glued together so the grains match exactly. Maple or fruitwood can be used instead. Swiss pine or spruce is used for the table, or belly, which acts as the sounding board and so is crucial to the tone of the violin. The head and neck are also made from sycamore, while the wood for the bridge – usually speckled maple – has to be capable of supporting the immense pressure exerted by the strings. The backs and heads of very old violins were often decorated with exquisite carvings, increasing the beauty of what are already magnificent objects.

Above: These walking sticks and badminton racquets were made in the 1920s. Some authorities believe that ash is the traditional wood for walking sticks, because part of the tree's mythical power and sacredness would have been transferred to the stick. **Facing page:** Oak is the standard timber for watermills because of its tremendous strength, although its high content of tannic acid will corrode any iron parts with which it comes into contact. Elm is used for the working parts that are permanently saturated with water because it will not rot.

Decoy ducks

Today they swim across bookshelves, mantelpieces, chests, stand on one leg on the floor or are dotted hither and thither around the house, but in years gone by decoy ducks used to bob up and down on lakes and the sea, enticing their unsuspecting feathered counterparts within range of the hunters' guns.

It was the American Indians who first created decoy ducks, moulding them out of rushes and mud and painting them with vegetable dyes to make replicas of wildfowl, although they were more concerned with reproducing the birds' size and shape than their very detailed plumage. In the early nineteenth century American settlers took up the idea, whittling the birds out of such woods as cedar and white juniper if they could get hold of them, or anything else that came to hand, such as blocks of driftwood. The practice of using decoys was most popular along the eastern seaboard, where game was a fashionable feature of society dinner parties, and it became such a thriving industry that many small decoy factories sprang up.

Hunters and fishermen were still whittling away at their own ducks, of course, creating regional and seasonal variations that would attract the migrating fowl as they crossed the country. Cape Cod, Stratford in Connecticut and the area around the Delaware River were particularly noted for their variations in style and are especially sought after by collectors today. The head and body of each duck was made separately and then carefully joined together before the

Just like their feathered friends, decoy ducks come in all shapes, sizes and colours. Some have tucked their heads under their wings, some have pulled their necks back in a parody of indignation, while others are craning forward ready to catch a passing fish. Many of them were carved and painted from memory by men who were experts on wildfowl.

plumage was painted on – some lucky decoys were even given a few feathers for extra verisimilitude. Actually, real ducks didn't care if their wooden counterparts were painted in only a rough approximation of their true feathering, but they would baulk at decoys whose necks, heads and bills weren't set correctly or who didn't float on the water properly: they had to look realistic, at least to other ducks.

There are two main sorts of decoy: those that float on the water (usually with their very own anchor and ballast to make them stay in one place); and those that stand on the land, on artificial legs. Often these shorebound birds, known as 'flatties', were two-dimensional. The craft wasn't just confined to America – decoy wood pigeons were frequently used in Britain and decoy waders were a feature of the Camargue in southern France.

Decoys were so successful at attracting their prey that by the early twentieth century some species were in danger of being wiped out altogether. Legislation passed in America in 1918 forbidding the random shooting of migrating fowl meant that the real birds were saved but that the decoys were doomed. Many little decoy industries went out of business and countless numbers of the birds were destroyed.

Today, decoys are enjoying a huge revival, but this time they are the ones that are migrating – across states, counties, countries and even the Atlantic as *aficionados* add to their collections.

Nineteenth-century and early twentieth-century decoys are collectors' items and are often priced accordingly, but such is the popularity of decoys that there is now a thriving industry making and selling modern reproductions of the old birds. In this photograph, six decoys share their perch with a fierce-looking chicken, masquerading as a wooden weather vane.

The Great Outdoors

Wood that has been allowed to
weather outdoors has a patina,
texture and character all its
own. The sun, rain, snow and
prevailing winds can all act as
decorative finishes, distressing
painted furniture, bleaching bare
wood to a fine silver and making
the wooden objects seem an
integral part of their
surroundings, almost returning
them to the landscapes from
whence they once came.

Outdoor living

According to Noel Coward, only mad dogs and Englishmen go out in the midday sun. The rest of the world, presumably, is sensible enough to hide away in a shaded porch or disappear into a rustic arbour where overhead climbing plants provide plenty of shelter.

There are many beautiful verandas and porches to be found, but especially so in America, where their basic construction is augmented with curved scroll work and all manner of decorative wooden finishes. The floors are usually made of simple planks or decking that extend from the house. They are ideal places on which to sit and watch the world go by, especially if they are at the front of the house: the interested observer has a ring-side view of what's going on but can retreat into feigned sleep or the depths of a newspaper whenever there's a need to escape the risk of detection. The roofs of both porches and verandas are supported on pillars, with the sides left completely or partially open to the elements. Even so, they frequently provide welcome wind-breaks and so can be used on days when venturing any further outdoors would be uncomfortable. Porches and verandas are also found on the sides and backs of houses, especially when there is an excellent view to be admired.

Balconies were popular additions to houses long before Romeo had ever heard of Juliet, and although many of them are made from brick or stone to blend with the architecture of the rest of the house, there are many that are simply made from wood, with decorative

balustrades running around them and planking for floors. In hot Mediterranean countries balconies are usually painted very plainly in cool colours so as not to distract from the view that lies beyond, nor to intensify a heat which is already considerable.

If a house does not already have a porch, balcony or veranda it is not always feasible to add one. A

Above: The view from this balcony is so magnificent that too much adornment wouldn't gild the lily so much as completely distract from it. The paintwork has sensibly been restricted to white and a creamy yellow, there's a deck chair to match and the panels cut out of the balcony afford tantalizing glimpses of the sea beneath. **Facing page:** The classic white fencing at the edge of this veranda doubles as a seating area for those who want to turn their backs on the lovely view and gaze at the house instead – let's hope it's worth it.

conservatory could be considered instead, in a style that matches the architecture and period of the house. Made of a hardwood that is either left bare or painted in a neutral colour, a conservatory serves several functions: it provides a garden room that can even be used in the depths of winter if given some form of heating; it can be filled with all sorts of tender plants that might not take kindly to growing outdoors; and it can act as insulation to the side of the house on which it has been built.

In a large garden, a summer house can look marvellous, and will provide a cool retreat on days when it seems a crime to be indoors but the glare of the sun is punishing. Roses, clematis, honeysuckles and vines can all be trained to grow up the walls and nod over the windows, and because the wooden walls would retain the warmth of the sun and provide some shelter too, tender fruit trees could also be persuaded to grow along it. Summer houses were particularly popular at the turn of the century and they deserve to be given a revival.

Rustic pergolas are a much cheaper way of providing some outdoor shelter. They can be large or small and are made of crossed pieces of bare wood. Specially treated lengths of hardwood can be used, or unpeeled larch, according to the style of the garden. Pergolas are especially suited to such plants as grape vines, laburnums and wisterias, so the panicles can droop down from on high and create a haze of colour.

Who says you always have to sit in the sun? This Scandinavian-style veranda has been made from lengths of unpeeled larch to blend completely with the landscape beyond, and would be very easy to construct oneself. To continue the sparse, spare feel of the veranda, the flooring is simple decking and the chairs made from wooden slats.

Desirable residences for birds

Dovecotes have come a long way. Originally they were rather basic and ordinary structures erected to entice nesting pigeons under their roofs. Sadly for the pigeons this wasn't for philanthropic reasons but because the pigeon eggs and the young unfledged birds, or squabs, could be plundered and borne off to be made into delicacies in the kitchen.

As the centuries rolled by and gardens became more decorative, dovecotes were also given a facelift. They could be painted, given tiled roofs, supported on stone pillars and even decorated with miniature flags that fluttered in the breeze. The inhabitants of these desirable avian abodes had also changed from pigeons to beautiful snowy white doves and fancy pigeons.

Today, dovecotes still look good in gardens, whether they are fulfilling their original function or are now home to any birds that take a fancy to them. Ideally they should be within sight of the house so the birds' antics can be observed.

One of these wonderful American dovecotes would make a charming addition to virtually any garden. Alternatively, you could have fun making your own from strips of hardwood and then providing a wooden, thatched or tiled roof. Don't forget such details as chimneys, tiny painted shutters, balconies, lintels, doors and even white picket fences because they all add to the effect. Once painted and allowed to dry out thoroughly before being placed in the garden, your home-made dovecote will soon be attracting birds looking for a suitable nesting place.

Shutters

An obligatory part of Mediterranean architecture and style, shutters aren't always so popular in northern countries. The cooler climate means people usually want to welcome in as much sun as possible, not shut it out. Nevertheless, shutters were often a feature of British and American houses built in the eighteenth century and came in a variety of styles. They could be made in hinged pieces to fold horizontally across the window, or they could be smaller, single panelled pieces of wood that opened outwards. Some shutters even slid up and down. When not in use they fitted into the reveal of the inside wall, and their basic design has barely changed since then.

In the Mediterranean and southern states of America, shutters are often louvred to allow air to circulate inside the houses but keep out the sunlight. They are painted in cool, light-reflecting colours and set off by pots of brightly-coloured plants.

Whether situated out or in, shutters act as excellent insulation against the elements, can cut out noise, and are an extra form of security against burglars if they can be locked or bolted.

Some exterior shutters may be more decorative than useful, perhaps increasing the width of narrow windows to make them look more in keeping with the rest of the house, or adding extra interest to an otherwise bland house-front. Decorative shapes can be cut out of them too, such as hearts, diamonds or half-moons. They should be securely fastened to the wall to stop them banging against it in high winds, whether they are purely decorative or not; and given handles so they can be easily shut from inside if they are to be functional.

Above: Shutters and their hinges developed in tandem with the doors of a house, as these simple country shutters show. The arrangement of the wooden boards closely resembles that on simple cottage doors. These shutters are so enclosed by the rampant ivy around them that they have probably long since ceased to function.
Facing page: This striking eighteenth-century Connecticut house, the Joseph Webb house built in Westerfield in 1752, has interior shutters in colours that contrast boldly with the rust-coloured weatherboarding exterior.

Windows and gables

Buildings have been given windows (from 'wind-eye') since the earliest times, to let in air and light and let out smoke from the fire, but they were unglazed until the fifteenth century. Before that, people had kept out the elements by stretching linen cloth, waxed paper or sacking across the window openings. In grander houses, parchment decorated with the family's coat of arms would be used instead.

The nobility and the newly rich merchant classes were the only people who could afford to install glass and, like everyone before or since, they made the most of such a demonstration of wealth. Vertical wooden mullions were originally fitted into the windows of timber-framed houses to help keep out intruders, but they soon became decorative objects in their own right and were often carved. Taller windows were made (to show off how much glass the house-owner could afford to buy) and horizontal transoms fitted across them.

Originally, glass panes, known as 'quarries', were blown by hand and therefore very small, so were made to fit into a latticework of lead, known as 'cames'. By the seventeenth century the glass quarries had become much larger, and by the end of the century sash windows proliferated throughout Britain and North America. At first the upper windows were fixed in place, but soon afterwards the pulley system, which is

Above: The oak jetty of this medieval building in Lavenham, Suffolk, literally and figuratively overshadows the leaded window below. The wide transoms and vertical mullions are clearly visible between the lead cames.
Facing page: Different centuries produced different styles of window, but one of the most popular and decorative was the Gothic arch. Here, curved glazing bars have been fitted at the very top of each window to form decorative arches. The windows are so attractive in themselves that they need no adornment at all.

still commonly in use today, was introduced.

The Georgian age ushered in bay and bow windows, and the style and era are now regarded as inseparable. Windows had been poky little holes for so many centuries that everyone welcomed the extra light and sense of space that this new style of window created, although in Britain a highly unpopular window tax acted as a considerable deterrent.

Polished sheet glass first became available in the mid-nineteenth century, and from then on there was no stopping the architects who leapt at the chance of introducing more light into their buildings. The previous Palladian principles of proportion and elegant classicism were swept away in the craze for bigger and better windows. Interestingly enough, there was a backlash against this fashion from the Arts and Crafts

Above: The architect who designed this barge-boarding was truly inspired. A barge-board is the board or screen that is attached to the edge of the gable of a house to cover the rafters and keep out the rain, but it is rarely as decorative as this late Victorian one, which almost looks as though it is dripping. The design of the windows has been kept very simple, to allow the eye to be drawn upwards without being distracted along the way.

Movement, who returned to the Tudor style of leaded windows and oak frames. Many medieval stained glass designs, using jewel-like colours, were reproduced in ordinary houses where they could be admired.

In the late twentieth century windows have become so big that they are called picture windows (though they often serve as doors into gardens) and may even reach from floor to ceiling. Sadly, existing windows are frequently removed to make way for them, sometimes taking half a wall with them, and many people find their bland lines and smooth outlines preferable to the more decorative style of french windows. In the country, many windows have remained untouched and unspoilt, perhaps due to lack of money, or needless change. Whatever the reason, we should be thankful for it.

Above: The ornamental moulding around this window is a drip moulding, designed to prevent rainwater running on to the wooden frame and rotting it in time. Until the early eighteenth century windows were made from oak or any other hardwood that was available locally, but then fir and pine were introduced. Their reduction in cost was offset by their failure to weather well, so the era of the painted window began.

Exteriors

One of the most fascinating aspects of travelling, whether from town to town, county to county, state to state, or country to country, is the different architecture and house styles you will see along the way. Houses are built on wooden stilts in many parts of the world, especially South-east Asia, China, Africa and parts of South America, to keep them free from flood waters and away from hungry animal pests. Despite such precautions, termites can cause immense problems in many parts of the world.

Wooden windmills punctuate the European landscape in a highly decorative way, so much so that many mills no longer in working order have been converted into highly desirable, if small, residences. The standard wood was oak, used for the windmill bodies, the waterwheels and the gears and driveshafts, although the heavy framing was sometimes made from yew, elm, pitch pine, ash or sycamore. Any moving parts, which had to be highly resistant to wear and splitting, were made from elm, while fir was used for the light windmill sails.

The most popular building material has always been wood, because of its cheapness, availability and strength. Medieval European houses (which are direct descendants of barns) were all built with timber frames, which acted as supports for the weight of the whole building; the infills, often of sand and clay laid over a latticework of branches, were there simply to keep out the wind, rain and prying eyes, and bore no load at all.

The fact that many of them are still standing a good three or four hundred years later shows what an effective system this was.

In Britain, it was the terrifying Great Fire of London in 1666 that raised the first doubts about wood as a suitable building material. The fire had spread swiftly from house to house and street to street, although it was not only the combustible qualities of the timber but also the close proximity of the houses that had caused so

Above: Even a short flight of steps leading up to a building gives it a sense of importance. Here, the stairs, coupled with the highly decorative porch, add immeasurably to what is actually a very simply designed and constructed Swedish cottage. **Facing page:** The School House at Hancock, Massachusetts, is a fine example of a timber-framed house with a very steep gable. The clean lines of the clapboarding and symmetrical windows illustrate the Shaker style of bare Classicism.

much destruction. Brick, and to a lesser degree stone, began to replace wood as the chosen building material, especially by the wealthy classes who have always been eager to show off their purchasing power.

The early settlers in America built houses inspired by the architecture of their homelands (although they were frequently building about thirty years behind the prevailing fashions) and their hopes for the future; but their ideas were shaped by the local building materials. For example, the Swedish, German and Finnish immigrants of the late seventeenth and early eighteenth centuries introduced the log cabin to America. It was a quick, easy and cheap house to build, although once erected it wasn't without problems. There was no way to protect the bare ends of the logs from the elements which would rot them, so they had to project quite a long way from the sides of the cabin. The houses weren't very stable, either, because they could only be joined at the corners, and driving rain and snow had an uncomfortable habit of forcing itself through the rounded logs into the cabin itself. These gaps were often stuffed with coloured woollen cloths or, in very poor homes, with earth and moss. Of course, there were other styles of building as well, and settlers were able to construct houses in the style of Queen Anne, for example, which were made entirely of wood. Later on, the introduction of saw mills meant great strides were made in the treatment of logs: they could be cut into rectangular planks, interlocked and given weather-proof

The intricate boarding under the gables of this house at Blaise Castle hamlet in England contrasts well with the magnificent chimneys, which are reminiscent of those made during the Elizabethan age. The dormer window, with its wooden edging, is original and was probably part of the servants' quarters when the house was first built.

joints, so houses several storeys high could be built.

The next change in timber-built houses came in the 1830s, when the Americans mastered the art of mass-producing nails. Lengths of timber could now be hammered together, and balloon-framed houses were constructed. The vertical members ran two storeys from floor to roof and were strengthened with horizontal, vertical or diagonal boarding that ran across the exterior of the frame. The houses were then given further protection with wooden clapboards, using redwood, cedarwood or painted softwood.

Clapboarding, which is a technique used throughout the world, allowed rainwater to run straight off the sides of the building and, because the horizontal boards lapped over each other, acted as draught excluders too. Oak and cedar boards were cut radially from logs to give wedge-shaped boards, while pine was usually sawn into strips, but all were nailed or pegged to the frame of the building.

In New England and California especially, the roofs were frequently covered with shingles – the wooden equivalent of tiles – which were arranged in the same way and were made from redwood, oak and cypress. Sometimes the shingles covered the whole house.

Brick and stone have taken over from timber as the most popular building materials in many countries, but wood continues to be the favoured medium in North America, with some beautiful results.

Above: The changes and innovations that were taking place in world architecture during the middle of the nineteenth century had their effect on American building styles. The Wax Home was built in Woodville, Mississippi in 1897, and is an example of the styles prevalent at that time. The two dormer windows and central balcony were designed to let in plenty of light, while the porch at the front of the house provided a shaded seating area during the heat of the day. **Facing page:** Simple clapboarding and wide shutters are the main features of this single-storey house.

Garden seats and benches

One of the greatest pleasures of gardening must be that of relaxing on a seat or bench in the garden and admiring one's handiwork. After all, even the most tireless gardener needs a break at some point.

It was the Romans who first made seats for their gardens, using marble or stone and carving the arms into elaborate architectural or mythological designs. Designs of this sort continued until the eighteenth century, when timber replaced stone as the chosen material. The seats also became much more formal and decorative, in line with the elegant and precise style of gardening that was practised at the time. A new fashion is always in direct contradiction to the one that went before, so the formality of the eighteenth-century garden soon gave way to the romantic movement, which was all in favour of woodland gardening and a much looser, more relaxed feel. As a result, garden seats became noticeably more rustic, made from logs, planks and even specially twisted branches. They can't have been very comfortable to sit on, but perhaps all the capacious clothing of the time provided some extra, and necessary, padding.

Many eighteenth- and nineteenth-century garden seat designs are still sold today, while others have even

Above: This hexagonal tree seat at Barnsley House, Gloucestershire, has turned green with age but that only adds to its attraction. When building a seat of this sort it is imperative to leave plenty of room around the trunk to allow it to grow during the years to come. **Facing page:** The Sunset Garden at Sissinghurst in Kent was so-named because of the sunset-like colours of the flowers which are best enjoyed in the early-morning and late-afternoon sun. This simple chair is an almost irresistible invitation to sit down and enjoy the sights and smells of dawn and dusk.

earlier antecedents. The famous Lutyens seat, for example, which is firmly associated with the English Edwardian architect Sir Edwin Lutyens, is actually an updated design from the seventeenth century. There are a great many other historic designs that are still in use today, such as the eighteenth-century barrow seat, with a wheel at one end and handles at the other, and the Windsor bench, with its gently curved back and carved frieze below the seat. Oriental designs, such as the Japanese Edo seat and the intricate chinoiserie of eighteenth-century Chinese-inspired designs, are also very popular.

The best garden seats and benches are those made from teak, cedar or oak, as these are good hardwoods that will weather well and not require much looking after. Try to avoid any wooden garden furniture that is joined with nails or screws and look for items with proper joints instead.

Another important consideration is where to place the seats or bench. You can use them as punctuation marks in your overall design, just as you would a piece of statuary, perhaps placing an elegant seat in front of a thick topiary hedge, at the top of a paved walk or to mark the end of a vista. Ideally, you also need something to look at when relaxing on your carefully chosen seat or bench, so avoid placing any seating where it will command a lovely view of the compost heap, dustbins or any other eyesores that you'd rather not be reminded about too often. On the other hand,

This plain bench has been painted in a deeper shade of blue to match the wooden planking on the wall and floor. Such cool colours come into their own on very hot days when they help to provide a haven. Painted surfaces like these look most effective when they've been lightly distressed, either by the seasons or by an artful paintbrush.

a low wooden seat placed near a pond would provide a marvellous vantage point from which to study its wildlife.

If you live in a very hot climate you will probably prefer to sit in the shade rather than the full glare of the sun, especially if the seat is surrounded by aromatic, pale-coloured flowers and plants that help to create the feeling of being in the middle of a cool oasis. If the seat is placed against a wall or fence, fragrant roses or honeysuckles can be trained to climb above it, or tubs of scented plants placed near its feet, to make a small arbour of delicious scents.

Sadly not even durable wooden seats and benches last for ever, but that doesn't necessarily mean they should be thrown away. Some lovely old seats were made in wide curves or delicate patterns and it would be nothing short of a crime to burn them or put them on the scrap heap.

Stone seats are often planted up with creeping plants, such as thymes or camomiles, and you could create your own version by placing a wooden seat that's seen better days against a sunny wall, removing the slatted seat and then placing a tall trough immediately below it (or supporting a short one on sturdy piles of bricks) and planting it up with your chosen plants. You could disguise the trough and brickwork by placing tall, spreading plants directly in front of the seat. Although you wouldn't be able to sit on it, you would nevertheless have a highly decorative garden feature.

This rustic log seat is almost hidden in the middle of a wood. Anything more formal would be completely out of keeping with its surroundings. Given a little patience it would be easy to make a bench like this at home, using lengths of unpeeled larch for the sides and back, and flat planks of a treated hardwood for the seat and uprights.

Entrances and exits

Doors are highly inviting objects, leading you into new rooms, houses or areas, but they can be miserably treated in houses. Anyone calling at a house for the first time will almost invariably notice what the front door looks like – could it do with a coat of paint? Is it smothered with knobs, knockers and other decorations? Is it a grimy indication of what the inside of the house will be like? Is it original?

House-owners rarely see much of their front doors, whereas neighbours, passers-by and callers will. Perhaps that is why many period doors that may not have been works of art but at least belonged to the style of house have been replaced by doors from a completely different age and type of architecture, with mock-Georgian emerging as the most popular, closely followed by imposing Victorian. Just one careless feature – such as a letter box of the wrong proportions or put in an odd place – can also spoil the look of a front door. Specialist shops and architectural salvage firms will happily provide replacement period doors, and some companies will even make a front door to the customer's specifications. Different styles of door hinges or brass handles are also available.

In the past, many houses with plain façades were given hoods or porches in keeping with the architectural style of the house. Not only did these porches keep the rain off visitors but they also gave added decoration to the front. They are particularly charming when decorating country houses, especially if they act as supports to

climbing flowering plants – it's almost regarded as a cliché to live in a cottage with roses growing around the door, but there's no doubt that such touches can add immensely to the visual appeal of a house.

Above: Nothing could be simpler than this white-painted batten door, made from planks of wood, yet it looks marvellous when given this verdant edging of ivy. This is a back door, but a front door would look just as effective when treated in this way, provided the plant is kept in check so there is plenty of room to pass in and out of the door without brushing against it. **Facing page:** The shape of this sturdy oak door is a sign of its Elizabethan times, when women's skirts were too wide to enter any narrow apertures.

CARING
FOR
WOOD

Caring for wood

Fall in love with wooden furniture and life will never be the same again. You will be unable to walk past antique or junk shops without going in to see what treasures you can find, and then you'll suffer agonies if you find a piece that you can't afford or can't find a home for. I vividly remember seeing a huge Dutch seventeenth-century oak corner cupboard in a restorer's shop in Sussex. It glowed and shone in the light and definitely had a personality of its own. In fact, I could have sworn that it winked at me once or twice, and it was only the sickening realization that I had nowhere to put it that stopped me whipping out my cheque book on the spot and no doubt bankrupting myself in the process. The restorer told me that it had been covered with white paint when he'd bought it, and he'd painstakingly stripped off every layer by hand until he reached the wood, which he then began to restore. And how – you could even see the original plane marks in the panels. I've dreamed of that cupboard ever since.

As well as being something to covet, that cupboard also showed me what wonders restoration can produce. Of course, most highly polished pieces of furniture have reached such glossy status thanks to centuries of hard buffing and loving care, but it is never too late to start restoring a piece of wood that has seen better days. Over the years I have amassed several wooden chairs, tables and so on that had been destined for the bonfire by friends or family until I spotted them, restored them and gave them a home.

Restoring and renovating wood at home

If you've ever watched an antiques programme where members of the public bring in their treasures for expert opinion you'll have seen some of the astonishing things people do in the name of restoration and repair. I know someone who has a most beautiful Georgian dining room table – but it's been cut in half to fit the shape of the room, thus wiping out its once considerable value. You can buy antique pieces of furniture that have been altered long ago, but strangely enough such emendations may not affect their value – they might even increase it. The trick is not to be guilty of any similar handiwork yourself, unless of course you really don't mind about carving up your lovely old Victorian desk to make two bedside cabinets.

Over-enthusiastic restoration can have equally destructive results, and I would always recommend seeking expert advice if you are in any doubt about what to do, especially if you know that the piece in question is valuable: amateur attention can do untold damage. Replacing broken panels, repairing old joints and the like really are jobs which are best left for the experts on important pieces, as are such tasks as removing stains, grease marks and the white rings left by water.

On the other hand, if you are sure you don't own something valuable (although it is surprising how often a piece of furniture you have taken for granted actually does turn out to be worth something), there is nothing to stop

you making some minor running repairs yourself.

Cleaning off old polish

Sometimes the grain on a piece of furniture becomes clogged with a mixture of dust and old polish, making the whole thing look dull and dirty. If you look closely you should be able to see the dirt caught in the grain, especially if it's a light wood. The answer is not to add another layer of polish in the hope of camouflaging all that grime. Instead, the best remedy is to completely remove all the old polish so you can start again from the bare wood – a job that is less daunting than it sounds, and immensely rewarding when you see the finished results. Once again, however, you should seek expert advice if the wooden object or piece of furniture has been French polished (which is a complicated

and specialized process) and, of course, if it is valuable.

First, you should remove as much accumulated grime as possible from the mouldings and around the handles with a soft brush and a duster. If the handles are easily removed it is a good idea to do so, as you will find it much easier to work on the resulting flat wooden surface. (Make sure you save all the screws and keep them carefully in a safe place.) Then wipe off all the old polish with a clean cloth dipped in a little methylated spirit, a proprietary cleaner or a solution of 1 tablespoon (15 ml) of vinegar in 1 pint (½ litre) of cold water (hot water may loosen old glue) and leave to dry – this may take up to 24 hours. You can now apply a high-quality wax polish. Many antique shops and wooden furniture shops sell a selection, but keep an eagle eye open for polishes that have a stain added to them as you might buy the wrong one by mistake. Pine furniture is best treated with an uncoloured wax polish.

If you want a very shiny finish you should apply the polish with a large wad of the finest grade wire wool, pressing down quite hard in

the direction of the grain. (Wear a pair of cotton gloves when you do this otherwise your fingertips and nails won't be the same for quite a while.) Go over the whole surface once in this way, then dust it off and buff hard with a soft clean cloth. If such a highly polished surface would look wrong for the style of furniture, you should just apply a thin layer of polish with a cloth and buff it well.

Stripping old furniture

In recent years there has been a tremendous vogue for stripped pine, and in some neighbourhoods it seems that a stripped front door and equally naked wooden interior are virtually *de rigueur*. Of course, unlike the Dutch corner cabinet I fell in love with, not every piece of painted furniture is revealed to be a work of art once its camouflage has

been removed, and sometimes after you've carefully stripped and scraped for hours you realize why the wretched thing was painted in the first place.

By painted furniture I mean pieces covered with a nice thick coat of gloss or emulsion, not the highly decorative ones that were made to be painted and are currently growing in popularity and value. They should be left well alone and taken to an expert for restoration, otherwise untold damage may result.

Doors and other large pieces are probably best sent to a professional stripper, who will immerse the whole thing in caustic soda. Some people make a complete success of burning off the paint on doors with a blow torch or electric paint stripper, but others ruin the wood by scorching it. One person, who shall remain nameless, burnt the paint off his window-sills and two hours later found them

smouldering (it turned out that they were completely rotten), so do be careful. It is largely a matter of personal taste and logistics as to which method you choose.

On smaller pieces the ideal is to scrape off the paint with a knife or piece of broken bottle, as this will not damage the natural oils in the wood. Take immense care not to make any scratches: it is only too easy to lose concentration for a moment and gouge out a lump of wood or lift the grain as a result.

Various chemical strippers are available for removing painted and varnished surfaces, preferably in one layer that can be peeled off, as this causes the least damage to the wood. Such proprietary brands are always best applied with a brush, but be prepared to throw it away afterwards as it can be difficult to clean properly. Don't burn it – both strippers and paint are highly flammable.

Strippers should be applied out of doors whenever possible. Always follow the manufacturer's instructions to the letter, wear some protective goggles and gloves and wash off any spills on your skin immediately. When you've finished, wash down the wood with warm

water and leave to dry, then wash it again using a solution of approximately 2 teaspoons (10 ml) of vinegar to 1 pint (½ litre) of water. Leave to dry for 24 hours before going on to the next stage.

Whichever method you choose, you must first remove all the handles, knobs, escutcheons and other devices that will get in the way, but be absolutely sure you have kept all the original screws so you can replace them afterwards. Any dirty metal can be cleaned and polished before being replaced, but don't make it too shiny or it will stick out like so many sore thumbs.

Assessing for damage

Once the wood has been revealed you can assess it for possible damage and take appropriate action. Remove any drawers and test their joints – if they are very loose you will have to dismantle and clean them, then reglue them with a special woodworking glue. If you discover any cracks or holes, these can be stopped up with one of the variety of tinted fillers that are on the market. Ask a reputable shop or supplier for advice if you are in any doubt about what to buy.

The next stage, sanding down, can be rather unnerving if you have never done it before because it seems so drastic. In fact, it is much less radical than it appears. Starting with a piece of coarse sandpaper, sand the wood in the direction of the grain. You may find this easier if you wrap the sandpaper around a small block of wood first as you will then have something to grip. Go over all the wood once, or until the surface is perfectly clean, then wipe off the wood dust with a damp cloth and leave to dry. Repeat the process

with a piece of fine sandpaper. Brush off the dust again and examine the surface closely for areas you have missed, or stroke it lightly with your hand to feel if it is thoroughly smooth. Go over any rough areas with the fine sandpaper, remembering to work with the grain. The more care you take over sanding the better the finished results will be, so don't rush it and try not to lose all enthusiasm halfway through as it will probably show.

Removing stains and blemishes

Very often stripping the paint from a piece of furniture will reveal a depressing collection of scratches, ink blots and water rings, but most of these can be easily removed. To remove light scratches, lightly sand with fine sandpaper dipped in linseed oil. To remove deeper scratches, fill them with wax polish and then rub them level with some fine sandpaper. Marks made by heat or water can be rubbed away with a mixture of equal parts turpentine and linseed oil, and the residue oil then removed by wiping over with vinegar. Bruises can be eradicated by placing a damp cloth over them, then covering with a hot iron for a few moments. A few

dabs of domestic bleach will remove most ink stains, but take care only to apply it to the stain and not to the surrounding wood, or you will cause more problems than you solve.

Now begin to rub a good wax polish into the wood with a large piece of fine-grade wire wool, always working in the direction of the grain, until you have covered the whole surface. Then buff it hard with a soft clean cloth – you need plenty of elbow grease for this. As with the sanding down, the more care you take with polishing the better. All the same, don't forget that the art of restoration is not to make a battered old piece of furniture look brand new, but rather to return it to its original, beautiful, state.

Of course, not every battered old piece of furniture can be restored so quickly or simply. You may

well be confronted with a chair that has lost its rush or wicker seat, a gate-leg table that is minus a leaf or what would be a magnificent chaise longue if only it didn't look like a candidate for the nearest rubbish tip. Such restoration problems go far beyond the scope of this book, but there are some excellent books available that will explain what to do in great detail. If you feel such arts are beyond you then seek the help of a professional, but make sure you find one who knows what he or she is doing. Just as there are hopeless builders, plumbers, dentists, doctors and anyone else you care to mention, so there are so-called restorers who are more interested in padding out their bank balances than your nineteenth-century button chair. Word of mouth is often the best reference, but you should also ask to have a look at some examples of

the restorer's work. Do the proportions look right? Has the underside of a chair been given its proper webbing? If the piece of furniture has castors, are they in proportion or are they far too big? If a new piece of wood has been used, can you see the join because the wood is a completely different colour? You don't need to be an expert to spot what is often just plain common sense.

Everyday maintenance

There are three main enemies of wooden furniture – heat, sunlight and a dry atmosphere – all of which should be avoided whenever possible. The ideal is to keep your furniture in a constant, cool and slightly humid atmosphere, but like most ideals it can be difficult to put into practice. Most houses have some form of central heating and that, unfortunately, is an excellent way to dry out all the moisture from a piece of furniture. Keep the furniture as far away from the radiators as possible, especially if it's valuable, otherwise it may well warp or crack in time. Placing humidifiers (they aren't all ugly eyesores) over the radiators, to increase the humidity of the room,

is an excellent idea and one from which you, as well as your furniture, will benefit. Strong sunlight falling on a piece of furniture will soon make it fade, so try to avoid this wherever possible. If you can't find an alternative home for the furniture, you will have to do something about the sunlight instead. Perhaps you could fit slatted wooden blinds over the windows, or clouds of filmy net or lace curtains to filter out the sunlight and reduce any possible damage.

Once you have restored a piece of furniture to its former glory, or bought one that is in good condition, the last thing you should do is smother it in polish again, especially if you want to maintain its high shine. Polish feeds the wood, but it's the buffing that follows that creates the shine. Always dust the piece before you polish it, to avoid rubbing in any

dirt, then apply only a small amount of good-quality polish with a clean dry cloth and rub as hard as you can. It's a useful thing to do if you're feeling angry, as it works off a lot of steam!

Painted furniture needs special attention and care. Never ever put anything hot directly on to a painted surface as the heat will not only mark the wood but also lift the paint. The same rules of cool, slightly humid conditions apply, and sunlight may fade the paint as well as the wood. Dust the piece regularly with a very soft cotton cloth but only wax once or twice a year with a special polish bought from a specialist.

You may think that one polish is much like another, but that's not the case at all. Most supermarkets sell a vast array of wood polishes, often in aerosol cans, but these aren't suitable for antique wood

which requires a special wax polish instead. Traditionally, such polishes were made from a mixture of beeswax, turpentine and carnauba wax, although many now contain some silicone to protect against scratches. Modern furniture is often given a polyurethane varnish, and an expensive wax polish would be wasted on it. Instead, you should use one of the modern polishes.

Dry and wet rot

These are words that strike terror in the heart of most people, and with good reason as they both affect the structure of buildings.

Dry rot is the most dangerous form of timber decay because it can do the most damage and can even spread from wood to masonry and plasterwork. It begins in damp or poorly ventilated wood, so is especially prevalent in old damp buildings, in cellars and under badly built flat roofs. The rot is carried by spores, and once they get going they will rapidly spread from the wet wood to adjacent dry wood, sucking the nourishment from the timber and making it so brittle that it eventually crumbles away. It also produces nightmarish orange to

deep brown growths and a characteristic smell of rotting mushrooms, and the air-borne spores can cause asthma, sometimes even in people who have never suffered from it before. Curing dry rot is a job for an expert, who will remove all the infected wood and replace it with new timber that has been treated with a preservative, as well as thoroughly sterilizing the adjoining brickwork or plasterwork. Equally important, the source of the dampness must be isolated and removed, otherwise the whole process will start up again.

After that, wet rot doesn't sound nearly so bad, and indeed it isn't. It starts when timber is saturated with water over a long period, but the spores don't spread very far or do so much damage. Once the source of dampness has been eradicated the wet rot will stop,

although the affected timber should still be treated by a professional in case any dry rot spores are lurking in it, waiting to pounce when the wood has dried out sufficiently to provide an ideal breeding ground for them.

Insect infestation

Sometimes it is tiny insects that cause all the trouble. In America, termite infestation is a major problem and requires swift professional help to eradicate the little beasts as quickly as possible. The death watch beetle is another uninvited visitor that repays your hospitality by munching its way through the structural timbers of the house. It prefers oak beams in old houses, especially if they're affected by damp or some sort of fungal decay, and the only way to evict it is with the help of an expert and a powerful insecticide. Some

wood may be so badly damaged that it has to be replaced.

The powder post beetle feasts on the sap of hardwoods, especially if they're your floor, and will often munch away until just a thin layer of sound wood remains on the surface, after which time the comic possibilities are endless (unless, of course, you're the one who suddenly does a disappearing act into the cellar or room below).

Another problem, and the one most people are likely to come across at some time or other, is woodworm. This is caused by the common furniture beetle: the females lay their eggs in crevices, cracks or joints in woodwork, and the young grubs that hatch out then start to eat their way through the wood – a process that can take up to two years before they finally emerge and fly off, ready to repeat the whole process on another succulent piece of furniture or nearby piece of wood, such as floorboards. The tell-tale holes that first alert you to signs of trouble are exit holes, not entrance holes. If you give the wood a firm tap and some fine white powder falls out of the holes, it probably means that some woodworm is currently in

residence, but even if this doesn't happen you should still treat the wood with a special insecticide. The young beetles hatch out between late spring and early summer, so that is the time to apply the insecticide.

All these horror stories underline the importance of having a thorough structural survey carried out on any house you are going to buy. For example, two apparently sane people, who decided to trust their own surveying judgement rather than hire a firm, both fell through the sitting room floorboards after they had moved in. *Caveat emptor* indeed.

Looking after wood outdoors

It's not just for decorative reasons that we paint wooden window frames and front and back doors; it is also to protect them against the elements. Therefore, wooden fences, gates, trellises and other garden structures need equal care if they are not to rot away quite quickly.

Many hardwoods that are sold today for use outdoors have been tannelized – that is, treated with a preservative that has been driven into them at very high pressure. They shouldn't then need any further treatment, and fencing panels, gates, trellises, pergolas and arches are all often tannelized. Otherwise, if you are buying untreated hardwood for any of these purposes you will have to treat it with a preservative yourself. This is more of a messy than a skilled job, and you should wear protective clothing, goggles and gloves and wash off any splashes immediately, whether they land on you or surrounding paintwork, as they will burn both. Take care not to splash any plants either, as at

best you'll burn their leaves and at worst you'll kill them. Allow the wood to dry out thoroughly before bringing it into contact with the plants.

Unfortunately many preservatives stain the wood very dark (although the combined actions of the sun and the rain soon bleach it to a more acceptable colour), so you might prefer to paint it. White-painted picket fences and gates are classics of country gardens and always look marvellous, especially when a host of plants tumbles over them. Many paint companies now produce paints that are specially designed for use outdoors and you might wish to use one of these, or you could use an ordinary good-quality gloss paint if you prefer.

When buying wooden outdoor furniture, teak, oak and cedar are the best woods to choose. They are certainly expensive, but their hard-wearing qualities make them excellent investments. The only attention they usually need is a wash down with hot water in the spring, although some old wooden seats and benches can become so dried out that they benefit from being washed down, left to dry and then wiped over with linseed oil.

Painted outdoor furniture often looks better as the years go by, as it loses its brand new appearance and begins to merge into the garden around it.

Renewable wood sources

Over the past decade the terrible destruction of the world's rainforests has been revealed in its true horror. If the current rate of destruction continues, most of the world's tropical rainforests will have vanished by about 2025, taking with them phenomenal numbers of animal and plant species and wreaking as yet unknown havoc on the world's climate and rainfall. It is a tragedy of massive proportions.

Just as there is no one solution to the problem, so there is not a simple reason for such devastation: politics, the advantages of cash economies, world debts and other matters all contribute to the problem. For example, the growing populations in such affected countries as Brazil, Nigeria, Papua New Guinea and those of South-east Asia are one factor. As more land is needed for housing, so large areas of forest are destroyed – often by wholesale burning, which creates its own set of ecological problems and means that the wood is wasted and isn't even used for building or export. For many Third World countries, the export of hardwoods to such rich countries as Japan and America is an important part of their economies, helped by the high world prices for tropical wood.

Efficient management of the remaining forests is seen as the way ahead. Countless experiments and conferences have shown that timber can be felled from forests without creating wholesale destruction. Of course, different solutions apply to different areas, but among the main ideas are that of enrichment planting, where native species are replanted in the denuded forests; selective clearance of fast-growing trees; areas around the main, protected, forest that can be used by the local inhabitants; and careful felling that does not cause the immensely harmful and damaging soil erosion. One of the major contributions that we can make to the problem is to recognize wood as a valuable and precious natural resource that needs constant replacement – and accept the resulting increases in prices.

There are measures that we can take, whether buying raw timber or finished pieces, and that is to ensure we buy wood from managed forests. Reputable wood merchants usually provide such information, as do shops selling newly made furniture. Ask if you aren't sure of what you are buying and if in doubt, take your custom elsewhere. In a market economy, you vote with your money, so give wood your wholehearted support.

Index

Page numbers in *italic* refer to the illustrations

Acknowledgements

Many people helped me during the production of this book, and I am grateful to them all. Firstly, my heartfelt thanks go to Gabrielle Allen, whose swift and good-humoured picture research produced a wealth of wonderful material from which to choose. This book would not exist without her. My thanks also to everyone at Ebury Press who helped on the book, but especially Fiona MacIntyre and Margot Richardson for their encouragement and help. Thanks also to Clive Hayball for his elegant design and support, Jane Newdick for solving what seemed a mission impossible and to Debbie Patterson for working her usual photographic magic. Thank you to the kind friends who lent me books when I needed them, and to Mr Johnson of Swaine, Adeney and Brigg for his time and help. Last but not least, I should like to thank my husband, Bill, who cooked countless meals while I concentrated on this book and was always a great support.

The author and publishers wish to thank the following for permission to reproduce photographs:
Bo Appeltofft/Camera Press: 121; Peter Aprahamian/Elizabeth Whiting Associates: 34, 39, 93; Bill Batten/The World of Interiors: 12–13; Boys Syndication: 9, 62, 71, 77, 80, 81, 86, 96, 110; Bridgeman Art Library: 28, 29, 30 below, 31; Richard Bryant/Arcaid: 79; Christie's, London: 30 above; Niall Clutton/Arcaid: 40, 78; Christopher Drake/Homes and Gardens/World Press Network: 59; Michael Dunne/Elizabeth Whiting Associates: 38, 45, 61, 105; Michael Freeman: 36–37, 41, 44, 57, 74, 82, 87, 97, 103, 111, 117, 120; Brian Harrison/Elizabeth Whiting Associates: 48, 58, 130–131; Jacqui Hurst: 67, 91; Rodney Hyett/Elizabeth Whiting Associates: 47; IMS/Camera Press: 92, 104, 116; Ann Kelley/Elizabeth Whiting Associates: 126; Lucinda Lambton/Arcaid: 55, 56, 112, 113, 114, 115, 128; Tom Leighton/Elizabeth Whiting Associates: 46; Claes Lewenhaupt/Camera Press: 90; Neil Lorimer/Elizabeth Whiting Associates: 72, 73; Stirling MacOboy/Camera Press: 123; Peter Marlow/Magnum: 83; Chris Mead: 32–33, 35, 63, 66, 68, 70, 75, 85, 89, 95, 99, 107, 108, 109, 124, endpapers and front jacket; David Montgomery/Homes and Gardens/World Press Network: 5; James Mortimer/The World of Interiors: 11; Ron Oulds/Robert Harding Picture Library: 64; Debbie Patterson: 14–27 and back jacket; Clay Perry/Homes and Gardens/World Press Network: 3; Julie Phipps/Arcaid: 42, 50, 51, 60, 100, 118; Walter Rawlings/Robert Harding Picture Library: 88; Paul Ryan: 1; Nigel Temple/Robert Harding Picture Library: 122; Peter Woloszynski/Elizabeth Whiting Associates: 43, 53, 65, 102, 129.